PRAISE FOR *THE SIX CO*
OF A BRILLIANT M,

'Every manager could learn something of real value from this book'

– Carrie Bedingfield, Founder, Onefish Twofish

'I recommend this book to new and existing managers who want to be successful and brilliant in their role'

– Dr Abi Layton, Research Scientist

'*The Six Conversations of a Brilliant Manager* is quite simply a brilliant book'

– Anthony Sheldon, Master Executive Coach and Managing Director, Mudita Coaching Ltd

READER REVIEWS

'Engaging and incredibly useful… I couldn't recommend this book enough to anyone who wants to get the most out of their people!'

'I really enjoyed Alan's book because it felt like real life not theory – easy to absorb and use. And they are just conversations! Anyone can have a conversation (even me)…'

'A great book that is easy to fly through… Really well laid out because you see the theory and the outcomes… Definitely recommended'

'If you need some help managing your team, and getting the tone of that conversation right – this book is definitely what you need. It will probably help with the teenagers in your life too!'

'This book was absolutely brilliant. The story line makes all the strategies clear, then at the end it explains when and how to use these strategies. [I] will definitely encourage my colleagues at work and friends aspiring to becoming managers to read this book.'

'I wish this book had been available when I was a manager. It's profound stuff but set out with clarity and in a highly accessible style. Those difficult conversations I recall having, would have felt entirely manageable had I known what Alan J. Sears has imparted. A must for anyone interested in getting the best out of their staff.'

'I found this book very engaging... The content is so relevant for managers and I will certainly be taking some learnings from these six conversations to use with my team.'

'Wow! What a great book... Great for everybody not just for managers!'

'The book really showed me practical ways of dealing with my day-to-day responsibility as a manager. No fluffy theory of leadership, just clear instructional advice to follow and apply to your own situation. Very easy to read as well.'

'This book puts some basic structure around key conversations to help make them consistent and effective.'

THE FOUR
FIXATIONS
OF A BRILLIANT
LEADER

A BUSINESS STORY FOR LEADERS
(and would-be leaders)

ALAN J. SEARS

Red Door

Published by RedDoor
www.reddoorpress.co.uk

A CIP catalogue record for this book is available from the British Library

ISBN 978-1-913062-72-9

Cover design: Rawshock Design

Typesetting: Sheerdesignandtypesetting.co.uk

Printed and bound by CPI Group (UK) Ltd, Croydon

CONTENTS

PART I:

THE STORY

CHAPTER 1

LATE NIGHT CALL

A week may be a long time in politics but sometimes it can feel even longer in business. It had been a tough week for Julie-Anne Johnson, and it was only Thursday. She was tired and she knew it. Her boss in the USA, Ted, was a good man and a good boss, but he worked on American time so his day started halfway through Julie-Anne's and his afternoon was her evening. Julie-Anne didn't like to complain, but Wednesday had ended with another long transatlantic phone call that finished at 11 p.m. She had been in her office until seven, got home at eight, having missed dinner with her children, and then was up early on Thursday morning to drive to Bristol. Heading up a division of a large healthcare company, she thought, might not be so good for one's own health.

Julie-Anne knew she could have asked Albert Chen to come to her office at the opposite end of the M4, to discuss how changing regulations would affect the division's marketing strategy but she also knew that Albert would want to bring in members of his team to explain their own thinking and ideas; it was his way of giving them credit. Albert also liked to bring people in at no notice for impromptu creativity sessions. All told, if Julie-Anne was going to access the best that Albert's agency had to offer she would be better off taking the long haul. As it turned out, the day had gone well, at least until she hit the evening traffic coming out of Reading on the way back. By the time Julie-Anne reached her home near Windsor, she had once again missed dinner with her children.

'Do you think,' her husband Michael asked, as she finished eating the meal he had kept hot for her, 'that tomorrow you might manage to be back for dinner and a chat before our children forget who you are?' Julie-Anne shook her head, but not in disagreement.

'I know, and I'm really sorry. You know I love my job, but I love you and the kids more. It's just that things are so busy at the moment.'

'Well I'm OK,' Michael told her, but I do think the children are missing you.'

'OK, let me work on that, I'll see what I can do – and thank you very much for my supper, it was lovely.'

The call came at 10 p.m. Julie-Anne rolled her eyes, put down her glass of wine and picked up her mobile. It would be 5 p.m. in Philadelphia. As always, Ted Williams was apologetic.

'Hi Julie-Anne,' he began, 'I know it's late with you, and I'm sorry, but this is something of an emergency.' Bad figures? Bad press? A product recall? Julie-Anne rapidly ticked off possibilities in her head but was caught out when Ted said: 'It's Rex, Rex Tillerson, he's had a heart attack.'

Julie-Anne knew Rex, liked him and respected him as a colleague. Rex ran the Imaging business of Incolumitas Healthcare. It manufactured and distributed a very successful product used, ironically enough, in the detection of heart disease. Imaging was a small division in Europe, and most of the people in it had worked together for a long time. Although the European arm was part of the larger global division, it still had the air of a family business about it; a helpful, collaborative culture where people got on well together. The news about Rex would be a shock to them.

'How is he?' Julie-Anne asked immediately. 'Is there any news?'

'He's been taken to hospital, and that's really all I know at present,' Ted replied. 'His wife called John Harris to let him know, and then John called me.' John was the Marketing Director for the division and not someone Julie-Anne knew well. There was a pause until Julie-Anne filled it, asking: 'So…?'

'I want you to step into Rex's shoes, at least for the time being.'

'But what about John Harris, or the rest of the leadership team over there? Surely any one of them is better placed than me to take over until Rex is back. I don't know the business at all.'

'I know that, Julie-Anne, but I think you have the qualities the business needs right now, and I'm not sure that applies to any of the rest of that team at present.'

'Well I'm not sure how kindly they would take to someone coming in from outside. What exactly is it you think I've got that they need so badly?'

At other end Ted paused, took a breath and then carried on.

CHAPTER 2

DOUBTS

'Rex has done a great job. He's been managing the business very well, but that's just it. The division has been a cash cow for years, we've known that, and during that time, good management was all it needed. However, it's facing big challenges right now, and the business needs to change. In fact, it needs to make a transformation – and that needs leadership.'

Julie-Anne took a sip of wine and thought for a moment. What Ted was asking would be a big challenge. If she said yes, she would have to start by getting Rex's team onside, and there was no guarantee they would take kindly to her coming in. For all she knew, any one of the team could have been hoping to take over if Rex had moved on or taken early retirement. They certainly all knew the business better than she did. And why was Ted so sure she was the right person? On the other hand, the very fact that he was asking her showed that he had faith in her. Ted Williams had an extremely pleasant manner, he was affable, sociable, always willing to chat, but he had hardly put a foot wrong in his career. He had surrounded himself with high performers, had a reputation as a shrewd decision maker and a great promoter of talent. Turning Ted down might not be the best career move she could make. Julie-Anne put the wine glass down.

'What is it you think the business needs, Ted?' she asked.

'I'll leave you to figure that out, but you know what I think: if you run a factory that's meant to make a thousand widgets a day and it's making a thousand widgets a day, what do you want to change? Nothing. Managers want to maintain the status quo. But if you need to make plastic widgets as well as metal ones, or your customer wants right-angled widgets instead of straight ones...' Julie-Anne knew that Ted had spent his college vacations building two hot rod cars from old and rusty wrecks. The resulting cars had gleamed, glittered, won prizes at shows and been featured in magazines – she had seen the pictures. The upshot was that Ted tended to resort to engineering metaphors to explain things, but she got the point. Imaging was about to be asked to do some very different things from the ones that had made it so successful for many years.

'And you are backing me to have what it takes?'

'Well I've seen what you have done with Esoterics and I think this would be a great move for you. Imaging needs your energy and positive attitude.'

'Nice to be appreciated, Ted, but a business transformation is going to need a lot more than some energy and optimism.'

'You're right there,' Ted paused and then went on, 'look, Julie-Anne, tell me if you don't want to do it, but I believe you can do it. You're right it's going to need a whole lot more than just positivity, but I think you've got everything you'll need to do the job. And I think it will be a great opportunity for you to show other people you've got all that stuff too. I'll be here if you want some counsel or advice at any time, but you'll be the one who has to do the job. What do you say?'

'Yes,' said Julie-Anne, 'I say yes.'

'Phew! Well Amen to that,' Ted responded. 'I thought for a minute you were going to turn me down there. I'll put out a company-wide email. I'll call John Harris first so he's in the know, and I'll tell him to expect you there first thing in the morning.'

'Hang on a moment, Ted,' Julie-Anne cut in, 'what about Esoterics and my team? I can't just desert them!'

'Good leaders have good deputies, Julie-Anne. Who would you put in charge if you were going on vacation?'

'Lynda Lawson, she's my number two anyway and she's very capable.'

'Well there you go. I'll make yours a temporary secondment for now, Lynda can act up in your place – assuming she's willing – and yes I know HR will want to dot all the "i"s and cross all the "t"s, which is both right and necessary, but that shouldn't stop us getting on with things straight away.'

Julie-Anne's head was so full of thoughts that she didn't hear her husband walk into the room as she said to Ted: 'Well, OK then,' not quite as confidently as she would have liked, and ended the call. She sat staring at the screen of her phone for a moment, then looked up and suddenly noticed Michael.

'I am assuming that was Ted, calling from the States, as usual? If not, I'll just have to assume you are in fact having an affair and maybe we need to talk!' Michael joked.

'It was Ted,' Julie-Anne paused, 'and I'm not sure I've done the right thing by agreeing to what he wanted.'

CHAPTER 3

MEET THE TEAM

The next morning was a rush but Michael's offer to do the school run helped. As a freelance technical writer, he was happy to flex his time around Julie-Anne and their two children – except when a deadline loomed. Then he insisted on complete solitude and massive focus until the job was done.

Julie-Anne arrived early at Imaging. She knew that Rex Tillerson had a reserved spot in the car park, but she deliberately avoided that. She parked a few rows back and walked across to reception. Although her pass would let her through the security barrier, Julie-Anne made a point of stopping and speaking to both members of staff on reception. They had seen Ted's email and wanted to know what was happening. Julie-Anne had to say she had no more news on Rex's condition and added just that she would be 'minding the store' for a few days. She also made sure she got their names, Patti and Frank.

The second floor, where Imaging operated from, was more spacious than it would have been in a central city location. It was bright and well lit, with natural light at either end. One end featured sofas and low tables, with a drinks area; the other had been partitioned into glass-walled offices for Rex and his immediate team, all except Naomi Wright, Head of Finance for the division. Naomi preferred to sit with her team in the mix of cubicles and hot desking that occupied the rest of the space.

The office had started to fill up, but John Harris had come in early too and immediately steered Julie-Anne into Rex's office. John looked to be in his forties. The office dress code was smart casual and John was dressed in khaki chinos with a brightly striped shirt. He wore tan leather brogues, which Julie-Anne thought might be a slight nod towards the 'smart' end of the spectrum.

'It's a bit of a shock, I must say,' John told her. 'I mean, I knew Rex was under a lot of pressure, we all knew that, and of course it may have had nothing to do with that. You could see he wasn't really enjoying it any more though. It felt almost as though he thought he had failed – failed the rest of us I mean – although that's quite ridiculous of course. Nothing that's happened could possibly be laid at Rex's door. I just hope he's going to be all right. We all do. I don't think he'll come back though.'

'You don't? Why not?'

'He's pretty near retiring, you know. Next year officially, but I wouldn't be surprised if he calls it a day. Unless he's up and about in a few days, that is. I suppose we'll just have to wait and see. Look, do you want a coffee or something?' Julie-Anne did, and waited until John returned.

'Thanks,' she said, taking the coffee. 'I can't help thinking that you would have wanted to take over from Rex, even if this hadn't happened.'

'Oh, no,' John smiled and shook his head. 'No, I don't envy you at all. I think you've got a pretty thankless task here.' He took a sip of his coffee then added, 'Look, I'll leave you to get on for now. I've got one or two things to clear up, but I'm only next door so just shout if you want anything.' With that John was gone, and Julie-Anne was alone, standing in someone else's office, with a cup of coffee and a sinking feeling. 'A thankless task' John had called it. Were things really that bad? There was, she knew, only one way to find out. She could look at the figures later, what she needed to do right now was talk to people and gauge the mood. Find out exactly what she had got herself into.

She had intended to start with John, but since he had made an excuse and left, Julie-Anne lighted on Naomi Wright.

'Oh hi!' Naomi looked up brightly as Julie-Anne approached her. Naomi stood up and shook hands. She was, Julie-Anne guessed, around thirty, smartly dressed in a navy blue pencil skirt with a jacket top and blue court shoes. 'Do you want me to run you through where we are?' Naomi waved a hand at a pair of screens, both showing spreadsheets filled with numbers.

'Actually, let's do that a bit later,' Julie-Anne suggested. 'Let's just have a chat first.' They headed for the seating area at the far end of the office, Julie-Anne taking her coffee and Naomi collecting one on the way.

'What I really want to understand,' Julie-Anne began, 'is how the business is. I don't mean the results; I mean how people feel about things.' Naomi looked puzzled and thought for a moment before speaking. 'Well, I'm not sure I know,' she offered. 'I mean my team are happy, I think,' she checked herself, 'they all get on well and we are very productive. We have to be,' she laughed. 'If the monthly reports are delayed even a day there's hell to pay, and woe betide us if there's an error anywhere.'

'And outside of your team?' Julie-Anne asked.

'It's hard for me to say, really. People are worried about what might happen, it's all a bit uncertain. I think people are getting on with their jobs and trying to stay cheerful. That's certainly what it seems like, but you would really have to ask some of the others.'

They chatted on for a while. Julie-Anne talked about her children and how they were doing at school. In return she learned that Naomi was not married but was seeing someone. Julie-Anne got the impression that, whilst not unhappy with the situation, Naomi might be looking for a little more commitment in the relationship than she was currently getting. Julie-Anne also did a little personal history exercise. She was careful not to name it, or to be intrusive, but by describing some of her own background, she was able to get Naomi to say a little about her own upbringing, and Julie-Anne knew that sharing such information was the quickest way to start to build trust in a relationship. As they were heading back, Naomi to her seat and Julie to Rex's office, Naomi commented 'It's very interesting, that's one conversation I have never really had with Victor. That's my boyfriend,' she hurriedly explained. 'He seems to clam up rather than say much about his childhood.'

'Maybe you should ask,' said Julie-Anne lightly.

'Maybe I will,' Naomi replied with a smile and a nod.

CHAPTER 4

BUSINESS YET TO COME

During the rest of the day, Julie-Anne spoke to the Medical Director, Vijay Shastri, and connected with Imaging's Sales Director, Jeff Reese, via Skype. Everyone was cordial, sociable and appeared positive; Julie-Anne learned a lot, about the business and about the people. Imaging seemed to have a great culture. It was early days, Day One in fact, she acknowledged to herself, so maybe it was no surprise that no-one was rocking the boat. Even so, everyone appeared to have high regard for colleagues in other departments and different parts of the business. From what Julie-Anne had heard problem-solving was a collegiate affair, people sounded very collaborative, and yet there was something missing.

She was still puzzling about it on her journey home. Something was niggling. What was that line one of the professors on her MBA course kept quoting? Finally, it came back to her: 'Every organisation is perfectly designed to produce exactly the results it is producing.' It had always sounded a bit too clever, a bit of academic showing off, but now it was starting to resonate. What was it that Jeff Reese had said to her? 'It's pretty much business as usual.' That was it. Business as usual. Everyone in Imaging was doing the same things they had been doing forever. Because the business made money, everybody just kept on doing the same things. It produced results, which the Group liked, so naturally nobody thought of doing anything different. And that was going to make change very difficult.

'What I have to do,' Julie-Anne told Michael over a glass of wine once the children had been prized from phones and games and were in bed, 'is *show* them where the business needs to go. I am going to have to paint a picture of what could be for them.'

'And what might be,' Michael added.

'What do you mean?'

'Well if the business doesn't change then it's headed down the tubes isn't it?'

Julie-Anne almost choked on her wine. 'There's no need to put it quite like that!'

'That's pretty much what you told me though. It's Dickens, isn't it? *A Christmas Carol.*'

'Now you are leaving me behind completely. What does Dickens have to do with this?'

'Think about it. In *A Christmas Carol* Scrooge is a very bad boss. He is miserable, overworks his staff, and the heating in the office is useless. He is also rude to everyone he meets and is generally a pretty unpleasant character.'

'Well I like to think I am doing a bit better than that.'

'I'm sure you are,' Michael grinned. 'So along comes the ghost of Christmas Past, and shows Scrooge how he has behaved throughout his past life. That does absolutely nothing to improve Scrooge's management or leadership.'

'No surprise there then.'

'No. It's not exactly behaviour-changing stuff. Then we get the ghost of Christmas Present. He shows Scrooge how he is behaving now. Still no change. Scrooge doesn't care.'

'People like him usually don't.'

'Right, but it's the next bit that's the point of the story. The Spirit of Christmas Yet to Come turns up – and this one is very scary. And he, she, it – take your pick – doesn't speak, just points. Now

Scrooge gets to see what is going to happen *if he carries on as he is.* Then he gets to see what his world *could* look like if he changes his ways. And bingo! This one does the trick. Here is the doom and destruction if you carry on as you are. Here are the sunlit uplands we can all go to if you are prepared to change.'

'That's it!' Julie-Anne sat up suddenly. 'I mean I like your Dickens story, and it's clever. It's the carrot and the stick rolled into one, isn't it?'

'Well I'd never thought about it quite like that, but I guess...'

'It's actually simpler than that,' Julie-Anne told him. 'I mean I can use that, it's a good idea, but the fundamental problem with Imaging is simply that no-one there has a vision.'

'And where there is no vision, the people perish.'

'Well you are full of glad tidings tonight, aren't you?' Julie-Anne laughed. 'OK, so I need to be the Spirit of Business Yet to Come.'

'I never saw you as a visionary,' said Michael, laughing too.

'That's where leadership starts,' Julie-Anne told him. 'Leadership starts with vision.'

CHAPTER 5

LEMMINGS

The next morning, Julie-Anne arrived early. This time she did park in Rex Tillerson's parking space. She wasn't entirely sure about taking up that piece of status, but just for a day or two perhaps a visible sign that she was there might be useful. Her first action was to email Imaging's leadership team asking everyone to clear some space in their diaries. John Harris was first to reply, but in person rather than by email. He poked his head into Julie-Anne's office with a smile.

'So, we are off for a spot of team building, are we? What's it to be – paintballing or go-karting?'

Julie-Anne could have been annoyed at that comment, but she wasn't going to start a new relationship by being sharp or trying to impose her will. Instead she smiled back and said: 'Neither of those. And while team building will be one of the outputs, teams develop best and fastest when they are working on real problems. So that's what we are going to do.'

'Real problems, eh?' John pursed his lips and nodded. 'Well we've certainly got some of those.'

It took two days but Julie-Anne finally had everyone available on the following Thursday and Friday, and had delegated the task of finding a suitable venue to the Customer Services team, who dealt with hotel bookings for visiting customers and for the Sales team when needed. She then set up a one-to-one meeting with each team member, starting with John.

'You said the other day that we have certainly got some real problems, John. Which are most serious, and which are most urgent?'

'Good distinction,' John gave his thoughtful little nod again. 'The biggest problem is Myovilite coming off patent.'

'Well yes, but we have known about that for a long time.'

'Not long enough to have a truly comparable replacement far enough down the pipeline to avoid the cliff edge, it seems. And when I say comparable, I mean that in terms of efficacy as well as profitability.' Julie had several thoughts in her head about that but said nothing and waited for John to continue. 'But even if Axxanent were fully approved and ready for launch, that's only half the battle.'

'What do you mean?'

John looked up across the desk at Julie-Anne. 'We have a very loyal and dedicated workforce,' he began. 'In Europe we are a pretty small operation, so most people know one another. All our field force are highly qualified. They are nearly all doctors; some of them have multiple degrees. And they like nothing better than going to the same hospitals and clinics they have visited for years, and seeing the same consultants and professors they have known for years and having lovely long chats about medicine. They haven't really sold anything for years – they haven't had to. Myovilite is practically an industry standard; it is well known, highly trusted and has approvals for use almost everywhere. I think when it comes to the end of its life that will be it for most of the field force too. They won't want to make the change, to actively promote something new, to talk to people they don't already know. I think they'll all leave.'

That left Julie-Anne a little startled. 'You mean they would go elsewhere? But who would they go to?'

'Oh, I doubt they would head off to the competition. No, I think most of them would retire, go and put their feet up, write the odd scholarly article, tend the roses. That sort of thing.'

'But that would be a disaster! We would have no business left!'

'And that,' John looked across the table with no satisfaction, 'is exactly what I am trying to tell you.'

'But I don't understand. Everyone has known that Myovilite would be going off patent for, well for two years at least, and that's when it was made public knowledge. I know Axxanent has been delayed, but even so, has no-one been thinking about this, making plans? Do we really have no strategy to deal with this?'

John paused then took a breath. 'Honestly, Julie-Anne?' She nodded, and John went on. 'I think everyone secretly thinks it's the end of the business. If they were being honest, most people would say they think we will either be closed down or sold off, although frankly I'm not sure what a prospective buyer would actually think they are getting, so how likely that would be I can't say.'

'So, we are all just lemmings heading for the cliff edge – is that what you are saying?'

'As a group, lemmings have a rotten image, but no individual lemming has ever received bad press.'

It was Julie-Anne's turn to pause. 'Did you just make that up?' she asked after a moment.

'No,' John threw her a rueful look and smiled. 'I wish I had but it was Warren Buffet. He was talking about managers and why most of them won't take a risky decision, even an intelligent decision, if the risk is that they could look stupid.'

'So, the intelligent decision here would be to decide to do whatever it takes to save this business and everyone's jobs in it?'

'Well, that wasn't exactly what I meant...' John paused.

'But that is the decision no-one is prepared to make, or stand up for, because everyone else will say they are stupid and there's no hope.'

'Well, I didn't want to put it exactly like that...'

'There's no need to because I've just taken that decision.' Julie-
Anne stood up. In fact, she almost jumped out of her seat. 'Thanks
very much John,' she gave him a big smile, 'that was a great
conversation. I know what I need to do now!'

CHAPTER 6

REASSEMBLY

Although the business was very keen to keep offsites onsite, Julie-Anne had won the battle with Ted Williams, and hadn't even had to try too hard. Ted had stuck to the corporate line for a few minutes before conceding that getting the leadership team united behind a real vision of possibility was essential to the survival of the business, and that was far more likely to happen if everyone stepped out of their normal work environment and got away from interruptions and intrusions for a day or two.

Julie-Anne had insisted on two days.

'Ted, you must have been on as many of these things as I have. You do a day together and at the end of it everyone goes home, then the next day you are all back in the office, and nothing much changes. However, if you do a day together, meet again in the evening, eat together, talk about other things, come back together in the morning, then things change. They really do.'

'Well, OK, yeah,' Ted responded. 'I know what you mean. I don't know why but there is something in that. What is it that makes the difference do you reckon?'

'I'm a business leader, not a sociologist, Ted, you know that, but it does occur to me that at pretty much any important point in life, people get together and at some point they sit down and eat together. Weddings, birthday parties, funerals...'

'Please don't tell me you are going to a funeral,' Ted laughed.

'Definitely not! I'm not sure what we'll call it, but it is going to be the start of something new. A new attitude, a new determination, but we need to go offsite, spend a day together, have a drink in the bar and a meal together, and then reassemble in the morning.'

'Well OK, you've convinced me,' Ted said with a chuckle, 'I just hope the team doesn't need *too* much reassembly in the morning, after the night before!'

CHAPTER 7

A ROOM WITH A VIEW

The Lakeside Hotel was only about ten miles from the office, but in every other respect it was in a different world. It was approached down a winding road with fields on either side; a stark contrast to taking the exit from the motorway straight into the business park, which was how most people's daily journey into work finished. A long, tree-lined driveway curved this way and that until finally swinging round to reveal what had once been the country house of a man who made his fortune importing tea.

The room Julie-Anne had chosen was deliberately large, a room people could get up and walk around in, and it had plenty of natural daylight provided by tall windows with a vista across the park and down to the lake. Julie-Anne knew that if she was going to get the best out of her team and promote some creative and above all positive thinking, then the setting would be all important. Tucking everyone into a small room without windows and seating them around a rectangular table only just big enough was not going to be conducive to either optimism or the creation of constructive ideas.

The team assembled fairly promptly. Vijay Shastri was first to arrive after Julie-Anne and he was followed almost immediately by Naomi Wright. Naomi headed straight for the coffee, asked the other two if they would like one, and poured for all three of them. John Harris arrived sporting a red and green striped polo shirt, greeted everyone, grinned at Naomi's suggestion that she might need to fetch her sunglasses, and helped himself to coffee.

A few minutes later, Jeff Reese came in with a self-deprecating story about the trials of family life with two teenagers from his first marriage and two very young children from his second. Julie-Anne had already picked up on Jeff's penchant for humour. Usually welcome, and she suspected often appreciated by customers before getting down to more serious matters, she also knew it was capable of derailing meetings, avoiding the point, and possibly being some sort of defensive reflex. Nonetheless, this morning Julie-Anne was grateful for it. She certainly wanted everyone in a good mood. And that was where everyone seemed to be until Paul Nettleton came into the room. Five minutes after the time Julie-Anne had asked everyone to be there, he walked in, nodded, said 'Good morning,' in a very level voice, sat down at the table and looked around as if it was the rest of the team who were late, not him.

Julie-Anne bit her tongue. Paul was a corporate policeman. Although Imaging had done nothing wrong under Rex Tillerson, and nor would it have – Rex's reputation for integrity and high standards was almost legendary – another, quite distinct, division of the business was under investigation. And that meant Regulatory staff were everywhere, with Paul Nettleton assigned to Imaging. What Julie-Anne could not understand was that Paul Nettleton acted as though he was there to catch them out, to prove something was wrong, when surely his role should have been to give guidance on keeping everything right? What made it worse was that any contribution he did make that was not directly connected with regulatory compliance was always negative. Any creative or constructive remark drew a withering or sarcastic reply from Paul, if he made any comment at all. Choosing her battles wisely and fighting down her instinct to say something then and there, Julie-Anne focused on the atmosphere she wanted to create and started to outline the objective of the two days and her thoughts on how the team could best achieve it.

'Our job, for today and tomorrow, is to create a new vision for the business. There are two ways we can do this. One is to go into a big consultative process, to run workshops and focus groups, put out surveys and poll people, then analyse all the results and come up with a vision from that information. I am not saying that is wrong, not for a minute, and in some businesses, possibly in this one at another time, it would be exactly the right thing to do. But all that takes time, which is a luxury we don't have at the moment. In addition, I think people are rather demoralised, energy levels seem very low, and there's no buzz about the place. I believe that as individuals, and as a team, we are liked and trusted by people in the business. What they are looking for is leadership, that's what we need to provide, it's *our* job to say where we are going.'

'So, you are saying that leadership starts with vision?' asked Jeff.

'That's *exactly* what I'm saying. Every business leader I have ever spoken to, at some point in the conversation, has either talked about where they are trying to take their organisation, or what they are trying to create. In fact, I'd go so far as to say the phrase I have heard most often is: 'what we are trying to build here is…' It doesn't matter what follows, whether it is about infrastructure, reputation, culture or anything else, whoever is talking has a vision of what they want it to be.'

'Yes,' Vijay began in a measured way, 'I can see that, but if what we end up with after two days here is some airy-fairy sentiment, you know, 'be the best we can be' or something trite like that, it won't wash with people and we will lose trust and credibility.'

'Absolutely,' Julie-Anne replied brightly, 'our job is to make it meaningful then!'

Paul Nettleton said nothing, for which Julie-Anne was grateful, but she noticed that he had pursed his lips and was already starting to push the Lakeside Hotel pencil provided at his place at the table around on his pad.

'OK, Naomi smiled in support, 'so how are we going to do that?'

'Well if we are setting out to go somewhere, it would be a good idea to know exactly where we are starting from. So, let's work out where we really are. I have seven questions for each of you, same questions for everyone.

- Who are the current stakeholders?
- What are the main external trends?
- What are the critical factors in our systems and processes?
- What aspects of the team empower people most?
- What aspects disempower people?
- What do we know?
- What don't we know?

Five minutes on our own, then we'll pair up and swap notes, and then we'll see what we have as a group.'

Naomi and Jeff opened laptops and started typing, John produced a set of coloured felt tips and started an elaborately colour-coded mind-map, Vijay and Julie-Anne made handwritten notes, while Paul, after a lengthy pause and several long looks around the table, eventually began, using the handwriting app on his tablet. When five minutes was up Julie organised the pairs. She put Jeff with Paul, reckoning that however negative Paul might be, he would do nothing to dampen Jeff's enthusiasm or halt the flow of ideas. Jeff could always talk for two people, and although he had an extraordinary ability to switch himself off and really listen to customers, it did not seem to extend into other areas of working life. Julie-Anne paired Naomi with Vijay, which left her working with John. Together they worked through their answers to the seven questions, filling in gaps in each other's thinking, amplifying ideas and adding in new thoughts as they occurred. The atmosphere in the room was good, even Paul seemed to be more engaged. Julie-Anne noticed that although Paul seemed to be so deep in explaining some point that he could to all intents and purposes have been talking to himself, Jeff appeared to have gone into his listening mode. She let the time run on until everyone seemed to have shared everything they wanted to, and the conversations came to a natural pause.

'OK,' Julie-Anne announced, 'this is a low-tech process. Let's get everything we have been talking about on flip-chart sheets where we can all see it.' For the next forty minutes the team shared thinking, noting commonalities but holding on to any outlying ideas, and creating a chart of answers to each of the seven questions. When the charts were tacked up around the walls, Julie-Anne said, 'Why don't we take five minutes now, without talking to each other, and just walk round all the charts and look at what we've got?' Jeff set a timer on his phone and they lasted about three and a half minutes before sign language began to take over, then somebody laughed, and in a sudden explosion of energy they all started talking at once.

'Well clearly we are not very good at the meditative silence,' remarked Vijay with a smile.

'No, but it was interesting,' John added.

'Yes it was.' That was Paul.

'Good,' said Julie-Anne. 'Well we have built a picture of where we are. Before we go on let's take a break and get a coffee.'

CHAPTER 8

BACK TO THE FUTURE

'Two quick questions to begin,' Julie-Anne said, her smile anticipating the reaction she would get when she asked the first one. 'Does anyone know the world record for the standing broad jump? That's where you stand behind a line and mustn't move your feet until you take off. What do think the record might be for jumping from a standing start? And let's make it easy, the men's record?'

Paul frowned. Julie-Anne thought he might be gritting his teeth for real and not just metaphorically. Jeff jumped out of his seat, stood behind an imaginary line and theatrically rotated his arms as if about to try it out. 'I reckon I'd get about six feet if I was lucky!' he exclaimed.

'OK, well let's double that for someone who is actually fit enough to do it,' John ribbed him. 'Say twelve feet then.'

'Good guess!' Julie confirmed. 'It is held by a man called Byron Jones, at twelve feet two and three-quarter inches. I looked it up just before we started. So, what's the men's world long jump record?'

'I happen to know the answer to that,' Vijay replied. 'It's eight point nine five metres or twenty-nine feet, four point four inches. Michael Powell of the USA at the Tokyo Olympics in 1991.'

'You should be in my pub quiz team,' Jeff told him.

'Only if all the questions are about athletics!'

'Or medical affairs,' Naomi quipped.

'OK,' Julie-Anne broke in. 'So, what's the difference?'

'About seventeen feet and two inches,' Paul said, rather too sharply for Julie-Anne's liking, but she pressed on.

'And how does the long jumper achieve that massive difference? Why did Michael jump nearly two and a half times as far as Byron?'

'He, or she, takes a run-up,' Naomi answered.

'Exactly! It's all in the run-up, isn't it? Byron walks to the white board, swings his arms and leaps. Michael turns his back on the take-off point and walks about fifty metres in the other direction to start his run-up. When he arrives at the board, he is travelling a lot faster than Byron and jumps a lot further. It's only an analogy but going back into the past first seems to create stronger, more powerful visions. So just as the long jumper turns his, or her, back on the objective and walks in the opposite direction which enables him – or her,' with a nod to Naomi, 'to go nearly two and a half times as far, before we start trying to go forwards from where we are now, we are first going to go back.

We are going to look at where we have come from – and what we have learned along the way. And here's how we are going to do that. We'll get back into pairs and complete another exercise. First, come up with a long-standing problem we have, or have had, in the business, but pick something you can define. Next describe its history, give us the back story of this problem, where it came from, how it has developed, why it likes hanging around here! But I am going to ask you to stick to the facts – be non-judgemental, and above all, no blame!' That got a laugh from everyone except Paul.

'Now you're taking all the fun out of it!' Jeff protested. Julie-Anne acknowledged that with a smile and continued with the briefing. 'Don't try to solve the problem, but instead ask yourselves how we caused it. That might be something to do with our systems or processes, ways of working, attitudes, behaviours, the culture of the business, whatever you think. Once you have done that, please be prepared to tell everyone the *story* of the problem you chose. Let's hear about the key factors, the main characters in the story, and most importantly, when you tell your story, I'd like to hear what you have learned so far.'

This met with some puzzled looks but after a moment everyone seemed happy to start work and heads went down. Even Paul appeared more animated, accompanying Jeff, who could not sit still for long, to the large bay window at the end of the room where an intense conversation developed.

I should have known Paul would enjoy talking about problems, Julie-Anne thought as she turned her attention to working with John. After a while the session started to draw to a natural conclusion. Naomi and Vijay, who seemed to have agreed their story first, continued chatting and then needed a few more minutes when a sudden burst of energy led them to a new insight they wanted to include. Paul and Jeff returned from the window still deep in conversation and both nodding, Jeff enthusiastically and Paul more thoughtfully. Julie-Anne and John finished off their story and everyone came together.

'Can we go first please?' Naomi asked, practically bouncing with enthusiasm.

'Well you look very keen!' said Jeff.

'Fine by me,' added John.

'It's just that we had a rather boring story, but then we suddenly thought of a better way to tell it!' Naomi explained. Vijay chuckled at that and said: 'Well, off you go then!'

'Once upon a time,' Naomi started, to laughs from around the table, 'Henry, Indira, Ahmed and Harriet decided to start a business.'

Then it was Vijay's turn: 'So they held a meeting and decided on their vision and values and their business plan.'

Naomi continued: 'They had all put some money in and it was a good business plan, so they were able to obtain some funding.'

Vijay added: 'So they had a meeting with the bank manager and a meeting with their accountants.'

'Then they had a meeting with their suppliers,' Naomi added, 'and a meeting about sales and another meeting about marketing.'

Vijay was warming to his task and with a barely concealed grin added his line: 'And the business was very successful and grew very rapidly.'

'And as more people joined,' Naomi and Vijay were both practically giggling by this stage as Naomi said: 'and more teams formed, everyone needed to have more meetings with each other to decide things and more meetings with other people to discuss things.'

Then Vijay came back in to say: 'And it wasn't very long before everybody simply went to meetings all day long, and nobody thought to ask, "Are all these meetings really necessary?"' Naomi added: '"And do we all need to be at all of these meetings?"'

Finally, with a quick glance at each other, they said in unison: '"And who is actually doing anything around here, other than going to meetings all day long?"'

'Ah! Very good,' said John. 'Yes, I like that a lot. The story, that is,' he added quickly, 'not all the meetings we seem to find so necessary.'

'Well, let's see what everyone thinks of our story,' Julie-Anne said. 'We are going to enter the world of mythology. It seems, and I have John to thank for telling me about this, that everywhere in the world in folklore and storytelling there is a cunning and mischievous trickster who often fools the gods themselves with his schemes, and by doing that wields more power than even the mightiest gods and kings – for which read senior management in our context!'

'Yes,' John came in. 'And our particular trickster has a very special name. He, or she, is called Workaround! Even more worryingly, the trickster Workaround is worshipped by many people here as a god. Let us tell you how this came about.'

'A long, long time ago,' Julie-Anne took over, 'there was a wonderful land called Imaging, where everything worked perfectly, and everyone was happy all the time.'

'And then a snake appeared in the garden?' interjected Paul.

'Oh no, something much more insidious!' John came back rapidly. 'This is a myth from many another culture to that one. This is a myth from where the Djinns come from, from the Ashanti culture of West Africa, from East Asian mythology, from the Basque people, from everywhere in the world in fact!'

Julie-Anne took up the story: 'So, at first in the land of Imaging everything worked perfectly. Then, although no-one realised it at the time, a clever trickster appeared. Now the reason he was a trickster was this: he didn't actually *cause* anything to go wrong, but whenever something did go wrong, he would whisper in people's ears and he would say something like this...'

At which point John took over the story. 'He would say something like: "Don't you worry about reporting that so that it can be fixed. That's only going to slow you down. You want to deliver, don't you? What you need is to find a way around this problem. Maybe I can show you how to do that..."'

'And so,' Julie-Anne came back in, 'with the best of intentions people started to look for quick fixes whenever an anomaly or a mishap occurred. They would find a way to get something done even if systems and processes seemed to be getting in their way. "It would be quicker if you just gave so-and-so the information they need, rather than entering it all in the system" the voice would whisper'.

'Sometimes the workarounds were clever, creative and even useful,' John carried on, 'but because they were workarounds only the people doing them knew about them. The knowledge was never shared or allowed to become part of the day-to-day for everyone.'

'Gradually people started having to work around other people's workarounds, although of course they didn't know that was what they were doing,' Julie-Anne finished off the story. 'And Workaround, the trickster god, said: "My work here is done, but I'll just pop back from time to time to make sure things aren't running smoothly!"'

'Oh, very good! I like that a lot,' commented Jeff.

'Oooh, yes,' added Naomi, 'food for thought there, definitely.'

'Right, I guess that's us then,' said Jeff with a nod at Paul, who began telling their story.

'This is a story you all know, but with a slightly different moral to the one you might be expecting.' Paul paused for a meaningful look at around the table and then continued. 'Once there was a hare who, even when he was very young, liked to run. And the more he ran, the more he liked it. So, he practised running further, and above all, running faster. And he practised fast starts and quick turns. Then he began to challenge other hares to races and he always won. "I am so good at running," the hare told himself, "and it is all because I trained myself to be so good at it. Now I am the fastest of all the animals, just as I always wanted to be."

'One day the hare was sitting quite still,' Paul went on, almost as if he were telling a bedtime story to a young child, 'when a tortoise came lumbering by. The hare found the tortoise very funny. "How can you be so slow?" he chortled. "Well I may not be fast, but I always get to where I am going," the tortoise replied gravely. "I can't believe you ever get anywhere," scoffed the hare. "Is that really as fast as you can go?" The tortoise was becoming a bit fed up with this and said: "Well, I'll tell you what. Let's have a race and see what happens."'

Jeff took up the story: 'Well of course, we all know what happens next. The hare dashes off but then decides to teach the tortoise a lesson, so he runs part of the course and then stops for a nap beneath a tree. He wants to show the tortoise how ridiculous he has been in challenging a hare to a race. And the hare fails to wake up and the tortoise wins the race. Now the moral of the fable is usually said to be that perseverance beats speed, but that's not always true. After all, if the hare had run straight to the finish line, it would have won, and perseverance would not have beaten speed. The real reason the hare lost the race is that he was complacent. And complacent to the point of hubris. He was so consumed with how good he was that he felt nothing could go wrong. And that's the moral of our story.'

'So, are we complacent, or prideful?' asked Vijay.

'We think we are very good at what we do – and we are very good at what we do,' Jeff replied, 'but we are a bit of a one-trick pony. We have refined and honed things to be very efficient...'

'Well, apart from meetings and workarounds,' put in John.

'True,' admitted Jeff, 'but even so, we do run a pretty tight ship.'

'Just as well,' Paul remarked.

'And when you get good at something it becomes harder to change.'

'Ah, OK, I see now,' Vijay said.

'Well that's three very good stories for us to think about,' declared Julie-Anne. 'Let's do that over lunch.'

CHAPTER 9

NOT SO FAST FORWARD

'So,' Jeff rubbed his hands together enthusiastically, 'on to the vision?' I feel like a bit of visioning after that lunch.'

'Well just hold your horses,' Julie-Anne reproved him, but with a smile. 'We have one more step before we get there. This is like baking a cake or cooking a good meal. First, we need to work out what all the ingredients are, or at least what all the ingredients are that we want to put in, and make sure that we don't miss anything out.'

'Yes,' added Paul. 'After all, you have just spent a lot of time working out how you create problems in the business, so before you get to a vision, you really ought to think about how to put all those things right.'

Julie-Anne noticed the use of 'you' rather than 'we' but chose not to fight that particular battle now. That one could wait.

'As we have seen,' Julie-Anne said, 'the problems tend to stem from systems and processes, ways of working, or things in the culture that we need to address. Which isn't to say we should ignore those things, but the vision needs to be more forward looking and inspiring than a simple problem-solving mechanism.' Paul pursed his lips but nodded a brief acceptance of the point.

'All right, so how do we go about this?' asked Vijay. 'Making sure we get everything in, I mean?'

'We'll start on our own,' replied Julie-Anne, passing packs of Post-it Notes around the table. I don't mean that we have to work in sepulchral silence, just that this will work best if we get everyone's individual thinking down first.'

'Empty our heads,' said John.

'Shouldn't take long then,' remarked Jeff with a grin.

'Well probably not in your case,' John shot back, good-humouredly.

'Here's the plan,' Julie-Anne continued. 'We want to get down on these,' she waved a packet of Post-it Notes, 'everything each of us thinks should be in the vision, everything it should encompass or encapsulate. One idea or thought per Post-it Note. And when we think we have captured everything, we will look at a way to bring all those thoughts and ideas together.'

When the last pen went down some time later, and the pads of Post-it Notes had become a large pile of individual notes at each person's place at the table, Julie-Anne explained the next part of the exercise.

'We need a large piece of paper for this, so we'll join four flip-chart sheets together with tape.' That done, Julie-Anne asked: 'OK, who has a nice steady hand, no artistic flair required?'

'Oh, I'm good at that,' said Naomi, stepping forward and picking up a flip-chart pen. 'What do we need?'

'A large circle, round the outside first. As big as you can make it.' Naomi complied. 'Now, imagining for a moment the circle is a clock face, join 12 to 6 with a line, then 3 to 9. Then go round and join 1 to 7, 2 to 8 and so on.' When that was done Julie-Anne added, 'OK, and let's have two more concentric circles – a small one in the centre and another halfway between that and your outer one.' When Naomi had finished, the team were looking at a chart something like this:

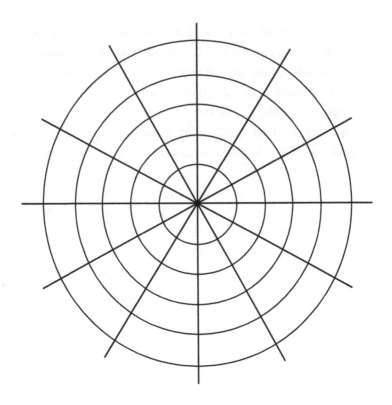

'Very nice,' commented Vijay. 'Now what do we do with it?'

'I think I can guess,' said John. 'We put all the Post-it Notes on it so that they are grouped up, using each of the twelve segments as a kind of cluster of ideas – things that seem to go together.'

'Exactly,' said Julie-Anne. 'You've done this before!'

'I've used something similar in focus groups,' John confirmed.

'What are the circles for then?' Paul broke in.

'The idea is to put everything around the outside to begin with,' Julie-Anne told him, 'and when we have sorted out the segments, to move the things we think are most important – the ones that will be most central to our vision – towards the centre of the diagram. That doesn't mean we will forget all the other things, we can take all the ideas back with us, but the vision needs to be focussed, and this part of the process is a way of getting that focus in place.'

Gradually the segments began to form into clearly defined areas. Similar ideas were grouped together until each section of the chart represented one line of thought around the future of the business, and what its vision should, could or might be. After which it was definitely time for another break.

CHAPTER 10

END OF DAY ONE

After the break, with its usual flurry of emails, messages and calls, Julie-Anne set out the idea for the last part of the day.

'We are not going to try to get to exactly what our vision is today. In fact, we are not even going to do that tomorrow.' That produced some strange expressions on everyone's faces, but Julie-Anne carried on. 'What we *are* going to do tomorrow is arrive at something pretty close to what we all think is right, and then we are going to take that away with us and live with it for a while to see if it really *is* right. And if it is, then we will make it real in the business.' That explanation seemed to quieten doubts, certainly no-one raised any objections. Instead Vijay asked: 'So what are we going to do with the rest of today?'

'I'm glad you asked me that,' replied Julie-Anne, 'because this bit is really important. What we are going to do is come up with every sort of analogy and metaphor we can that will help us explore and integrate everything we have on the chart so far. If anyone is feeling artistic, then pictures, cartoons, sketches, anything like that would be great. And above all – stories. Stories about other people's visions, and I don't just mean other businesses, but people you know, or have known, who had a vision of doing something, achieving something or creating something, and made it happen. All things that will bring our ideas alive and make what we are trying to do here seem much less of an exercise and something vital and important to us all.'

'Well of course,' Jeff put in, 'athletes use visioning all the time to pull them towards where they want to be. There's a particularly good story about a pole vaulter sitting in the stands of a stadium during a training session. His coach walks up and asks him why he isn't training. "I am," the vaulter replies. "Doesn't look like it to me," responds the coach. "Well, you see that bar?" the vaulter asks. The coach looks over his shoulder and sees the pole vault bar, way up in the air, looking impossibly high, as it always does. "Yes," says the coach. "Well, it's gone up three times since I started doing this. The officials have just raised it to a new world record height, and I am about to clear it!"'

'So, if I've got this right,' Naomi said, 'the link is that a good, strong and inspiring vision will help us do exceptional things by sort of pulling us towards it?'

'That's it,' agreed Vijay. 'Although when athletes do it, they may well be strengthening some of the same neural pathways that they actually use in their event, just by thinking about it, so that wouldn't be the same. But if we can all agree about where we want the business to go, or what we want it to become, and we all hold on to that, then it is much more likely that we will get there.'

'All sounds very new-age, self-help, and if you don't mind my saying so, a bit delusional to me,' Paul put in. 'If you are telling me that I can make something happen just by thinking about it, I put about as much faith in that as I do in remote viewing or telekinesis.'

'Well, no, there isn't much you can do by just thinking about things, apart from theoretical physics maybe,' John suggested, 'but maybe the thought is father to the action.'

'Or mother,' Naomi put in. 'You could see thoughts as giving birth to actions. If you chose to.'

'Yes,' Vijay agreed. 'And you can spend all day on the web looking at other companies' visions but after a few they tend to be incredibly repetitive. The best vision I know of is the Alzheimer's Association's.'

'And what is it?' asked John.

'*A world without Alzheimer's*,' Vijay told him with a smile.

'I should have thought of that,' said John, adding: 'In fact, I wish I had thought of it!'

'I like the North Star idea,' Naomi said. 'Firstly it gives everyone a clear understanding of the direction we want to go in, but also if you think of a simple representation of a star, one with four or five points, then you can incorporate a number of different ideas, like great place to work as well as great customer service, for example.'

'That's sort of what we've got, isn't it?' Vijay asked. 'I mean with the slices of pizza, or the segments of the wheel, or whatever we are calling them.'

'Yes, it is,' said Julie-Anne, 'but we have too many there to list them all. What we need to do is link things together where we can, while deciding which things are most important.'

'Well let's do that,' John said, getting up and moving to the chart on the wall.

'Yes, OK, but there's a couple of guidelines,' Julie-Anne said. 'Firstly, no wordsmithing is allowed at this point, along with any efforts to try and write sentences, paragraphs or vision statements.'

'I thought that was what we were all here to do,' sniffed Paul.

'It is, but not at this stage.' Julie-Anne went on, 'I'll explain why, but the second no-no is trying to remove contradictions or watering down any of the points to include all shades of opinion. The reason for both those rules is that doing those things tends to remove creativity and originality. Then we will be in danger of ending up with a dull and meaningless statement that could be applied to any team in any business – in which case, it is not really a vision.

'Our job for now is to agree on a number of bullet points – even if they are inelegant, ungrammatical and contradictory. Then we can talk about them, discuss them and refine them. If we had more time, I would suggest we go off and live with them for a month before trying to come up with one unifying statement, but time is a luxury we don't have. What we do have is the opportunity to do this piece now, keep talking over dinner and come back tomorrow with fresh minds and a sharp focus.'

With general agreement everyone clustered around the chart and a lively discussion soon began. Gradually several overarching themes began to emerge.

'Let's get some of these written up,' Vijay suggested, and Naomi wrote on a separate flip-chart sheet:

- Great customer service
- The best possible experience for patients
- Sustainability
- Excellence
- Great place to work

'That doesn't look very exciting, or frankly, sound very original,' said Paul.

'Maybe not,' Julie-Anne said, 'but that's the next part of the process. What we have done here is decide on the underpinnings, the foundations if you like. And that's very important.'

Paul did not seem exactly mollified by that but said no more, and with an agreement to meet in the bar for a drink before dinner, the team called it a day and dispersed.

Back in her room, Julie-Anne called Michael.

'How's it going?' he asked.

'Pretty good, I think. Paul Nettleton is being his usual obstreperous self, but everyone else is working well together and I think we are getting somewhere. Have you had a good day?'

'Workwise pretty good, yes, but Olivia has been in a sulk ever since she got back from school and Jason has disappeared to his room, no doubt deep into Minecraft, or whatever it is he is playing, so not great on the family front.'

'Oh dear, any idea why?'

'None whatsoever,' Michael replied, 'unless it's a response to becoming a single parent family.'

'Woah! That's a bit harsh!' Julie-Anne felt quite stung.

'Not my view, you understand, but I think that's what I am meant to take from it.'

'Well, OK,' Julie-Anne calmed down a little. 'Let's talk about it when I get back tomorrow. I am not going back into the office when we finish here, so for once I will be home in good time.'

'I shall look forward to that very much,' Michael told her. 'Now I am going to make some supper. You enjoy your team dinner and I'll see you tomorrow.' And with that he signed off, leaving Julie-Anne to worry about her children on her own.

CHAPTER 11

LOOKING AHEAD

Different morning routines resulted in only Naomi and Julie-Anne breakfasting together; Naomi after swimming twenty minutes in the hotel pool and Julie-Anne making a late start having slept badly. Vijay ate early and went back to his room to catch up on emails. Paul was in the gym, while Jeff and John had paired up for an early morning run. By nine o'clock though everybody was back in the conference room ready for day two.

'So, we have got a lot of statements about what we want the business to be and how we want it to be, and identified some major themes behind those things,' Julie-Anne began. 'What I would like us to do now is to take ten minutes on our own and project our thinking, or perhaps more accurately our imaging –' Jeff laughed at that. 'Pun intended,' Julie-Anne assured him, ' – into the future. I'm not going to put a timescale on that, but I suggest we think in terms of the current situation, meaning that going too far into the future is probably not helpful.

'What I do want us to focus on is what the very best organisation, doing what we do, could possibly look like. We need to dream a little here and expand our minds. Remove the barriers, the "can't-dos" and the "that-won't-happens", and build a positive picture of everything great we would like to be.'

With a few nods and agreements everyone set to work, Vijay sitting back in his chair, Jeff pacing, Naomi head down and thoughtful, John staring into the middle distance and Paul walking to the window to look out over the parkland behind the hotel.

When the ten minutes was up, the team gathered back at the table and began to share their ideas of what the future might look like. It soon became apparent that everyone's ideas were very similar, proving the value of all the preparatory work on the previous day. It was Vijay who pointed out that of the five bullet points they had arrived at the evening before, sustainability, excellence and being a great place to work could be classified as internal, whilst great customer service and providing the best possible experience for patients were about the external world. There was general agreement that the vision needed to encompass both.

There was a lot of discussion about what 'excellent' meant, or should mean, and about whether a focus on sustainability should, like being an ethical organisation, simply be a given. Julie-Anne noticed John tapping away at his phone. Phones were supposed to be switched off during the session, but she was slow to issue a reprimand. After a few moments, John looked up and held his phone up, the screen facing out towards the table.

'What we need to be is a *brilliant* organisation!' he said with a big smile. 'I've checked a few synonyms – and they included excellent, so it captures that. It also includes being first-rate, first-class, accomplished, inventive, creative, expert (which we are already), talented, bright, and clever!'

'Brilliant!' said Naomi. 'I like that. I like that a lot.'

'There's a whole lot more,' John announced, 'but you get the idea!'

'Seems quite all encompassing,' said Paul. 'Will we need to issue everyone a thesaurus to go with it?'

Vijay laughed at that. 'I think people have a pretty good idea of something being brilliant. And who wouldn't want to say that where they work is brilliant? Seems good to me. What do you think Julie-Anne?' he asked.

'I think it's brilliant too,' she laughed. 'Jeff?'

'Oh, I'm in, definitely,' said Jeff, 'I'm all for being part of a brilliant organisation.'

Whilst avoiding Paul's thesaurus suggestion, the focus turned to having agreement in the team about what a brilliant organisation would include, and that took them back to the detail points on their wheel diagram. Eventually the team concluded that a brilliant organisation would of course operate in a sustainable fashion, be ethically run and socially conscious. It would be a great place to work, one that would provide opportunities for development to all, while contributing on a broader front to its community at large. Eventually, happy that they could each individually justify and explain the organisational vision, the team switched their attention to the external perspective.

They talked about health trusts and clinics, about cardiologists and patients, about the different healthcare systems in different countries, and everything they tried to formulate became increasingly wordy and overblown.

'You know,' Vijay said at last, 'I've been in a lot of these discussions over the years, about who the customer is. Is it the person in charge of procurement? Is it whoever is paying the bill? Is it the person or the team who are using the product? Or is it the patient who benefits from it? And the answer is, you can make a case for all of those. I think what we need is something that encompasses all of those groups and says in a simple way that what they are going to get from us is the best product and best service it is possible to offer.'

'Best in class then?' proposed Naomi, and suddenly the deadlock was broken.

'A best-in-class imaging service delivered by a brilliant organisation?' Julie-Anne suggested.

'You know, I had never thought about it before but that is exactly what we should be aiming at,' said Jeff.

'It has the merit of being succinct,' was as far as Paul was prepared to go, but the rest of the team were enthusiastic in immediately adopting it.

The morning had flown by and the team broke for lunch. Julie-Anne was pleased, and very relieved, to see the obvious uplift in energy that creating a vision everyone could get behind had produced. In response to Jeff's cheery enquiry: 'Now that we've done that can we all go back to the office?' she said: 'Not quite yet, Jeff, there's a bit more work to do about how we are going to communicate the vision, and how we are going to stand behind it and make it real.' Which provided plenty of work for the afternoon session.

CHAPTER 12

HOME TRUTHS

Flushed with success at the results of the leadership team offsite, thrilled to be getting home early for once, and looking forward to some time with her children, Julie-Anne opened her front door and suddenly felt more like a war correspondent landing in a battle zone.

Michael was visibly stressed. Olivia, fourteen, and trying to find her feet, was being loudly bossy, and her brother Jason, younger by two years, was having none of being shouted down by his big sister. Julie-Anne's pleas for calm fell on deaf ears. She had only been in the house a few minutes when Michael shouted; Olivia slammed the table with both hands, grabbed her phone and stormed out; and Jason instantly began a very noisy protest that his sister was a pain, he didn't want to have a sister at all, and none of what had happened was his fault. As Julie-Anne tried to say something, Jason glared at her and muttered: 'Going to my room.' Then he too was gone.

Julie-Anne looked aghast at Michael.

'What on earth's been going on?' she asked.

'Oh, you tell me,' responded Michael. 'I don't know what's got into them both. They've been sulky, moody and generally difficult the whole time you've been away.'

'You're not suggesting it is because they were missing me?'

'Sadly no, that would be all too simple, logical and reasonable. Reasonable is one thing neither of them is being.'

'Let's give them both a few minutes then I'll go and have a word. At least see if I can get them to come and sit at the table for a meal.'

'Fair enough,' said Michael, without making it sound fair at all. 'I was intending to make pasta carbonara, supposedly everyone's favourite around here. Kind of "welcome home, Mum".'

'I have only been away for one night,' Julie-Anne was gently reproving, but her tone was light.

'Well, that's enough for welcome-home pasta, isn't it? I wasn't offering a five-course gourmet dinner with a wine flight.' Michael poured a glass of wine for Julie-Anne, who noticed that he already had one half drunk.

'It's a bit early isn't it,' she commented lightly, accepting the drink.

Michael shrugged. 'Let's just call it a celebration,' he said, but it didn't sound like one.

A little while later, Julie-Anne headed up to see Olivia.

'OK Livvy,' she started. 'What's up?'

'Nothing,' Olivia replied, staring down at her phone, thumbs flicking as she scrolled up and down. Not a good time to try parental authority or demand complete attention, Julie-Anne thought. No phones or laptops in meetings was a good rule in business as far as she was concerned, but parenting required a slightly different skill set.

She tried again. 'That wasn't the happiest household scene I came in to.' She let that hang. One thing Julie-Anne did know about was the power of silence in conversation. And although it was Olivia who held the distraction of her phone in her hands, it was Olivia who broke the tension first.

'It's Dad,' she snapped. 'Telling me what to do, or what not to do more likely, all the time. And Jason keeps bugging me. He's a pest and I don't want him around.'

'Well, OK, but that could be a bit tricky. He is your brother, and he is only twelve so we can hardly throw him out of the house.'

'Oh!' Olivia shouted, throwing her phone down onto the bed beside her. 'Don't be so *stupid*! You know that's not what I meant!'

Julie-Anne ignored the insult, fought back all the thoughts about what would have happened to her if she had talked to her mother like that, and asked: 'So what did you mean?'

'I don't know!' was Olivia's, by now slightly tearful, response.

'Well, I'll give you a hug if you want one.' Julie-Anne knew there was no chance of Olivia accepting, but it was a peace offering and she thought it might register as such.

Shortly afterwards she was with Jason, equally as tearful and rather whinier but telling the same story. In his case amplified by his big sister being bossy.

Julie-Anne's efforts at reconciliation resulted in everyone being present at the family supper, but although any major eruptions were avoided, it was not a very cheery occasion. When the children had gone up to bed that evening, Julie-Anne sat with a morose Michael.

'Maybe I'm just a lousy father! I do try but they just fight and squabble, they don't do what they're asked, and I lose my temper.'

'You know what I think?'

'No!'

'I think everyone here is staring down at their boots. What we need is a bit more vision, we need a family offsite.'

'You are not seriously suggesting we go off to some conference centre like you do with your teams and play about with planks and ropes or whatever it is you get up to at those things?'

Julie laughed. 'We don't do planks or ropes! We don't go canoeing up trees as my old boss used to call it, and I have never done a course in Leadership by Lion Taming – which one of my current team was fearful we might do. He was being sarcastic, of course.'

'That would be your Mr Nettleton, I presume? The thorn in your side.'

'Well, yes, but you know, even he has come round a lot in these last two days, and that's really my point. What we did was spend two days working out where we want to go as a team, and where we want to take the business. If we hadn't agreed on that, we would all be pulling in different directions, even if not deliberately. We need something like that as a family, something to draw us all together a bit.'

'Are you suggesting we have some sort of family vision or mission statement? Because I can tell you I am not going within a million miles of anything like that!'

'No, no, no. Even in the business it's not the words that are important, they are merely a way of communicating the idea. It's the *idea* of where we are going or what we are trying to build that's important.'

Michael took another drink of wine, stayed quiet and looked thoughtful. Julie-Anne waited. Eventually Michael put down his glass, looked at her and asked: 'So what do you have in mind?'

'Ah,' said Julie-Anne, 'now you are asking! What would be a really great idea for a proper day out that will raise everyone's spirits and make us feel like a family again?'

CHAPTER 13

A DEALER IN HOPE

The next week at work took off in a flurry of meetings. Product meetings followed sales meetings and marketing meetings, medical affairs demanded attention, and Paul Nettleton sat in his office sending less than helpful emails, checking compliance, looking for faults as Julie-Anne saw it. By Wednesday evening she was not only tired, she could see her plan to rejuvenate Imaging falling at the first hurdle.

Friday afternoon was a leadership team meeting though. Julie-Anne had changed the way this meeting was run. She had scrapped the preprepared and circulated agenda in favour of a rapid round-the-table download from everyone, no more than one minute per person, of the most important things on each person's mind. Those items, or at least the ones concerning the whole team, then formed the agenda.

This transformed the meeting from a blamestorm, with everyone wanting to suggest to everyone else what they should be doing or suggesting ways to do things without fully understanding the issues, into a positive, fast-paced session. People reported progress against targets, mentioned issues they were dealing with but did not need help with, and asked for discussion and suggestions in areas where they wanted help, with the problem well explained and listened to before anyone was allowed to propose a solution.

On Thursday morning Julie-Anne emailed her team to say that this Friday's meeting would be a little different. There would be one agenda item, chosen by her. Response ranged from Naomi's 'Intriguing!' to Paul's tart enquiry about whether this would be an ongoing change, together with a request for an agenda, even though Julie-Anne had said she would not be issuing one. As far as other calls on her time allowed, she spent time preparing. It was, she reflected, an interesting challenge. She was about to ask her team to do something they clearly had not been used to doing, and something she had never thought very clearly about herself. It was something she had seen other people do, and she had dared to hope that she might do it herself; Friday's meeting would be the test of that.

CHAPTER 14

SECOND SURPRISE

Thursday evening at home showed a small improvement, mainly because Olivia and Jason seemed too fed up to bother arguing, with each other or with their parents. Julie-Anne took charge of the kitchen. Lentil lasagne with a side salad for Olivia, and Julie-Anne would have that too; shepherd's pie for Michael and Jason, Michael's with red cabbage, Jason's with baked beans. With a rueful reflection on her childhood suppers of one meal for all the family, Julie-Anne set about keeping everyone happy in an effort to get some sort of harmony for her announcement about the weekend.

Frozen yoghurt followed, generally a sure-fire winner, and it did not disappoint.

'Just before you all disappear,' Julie-Anne seized the moment, 'we are all going out on Saturday.'

'We are?' Michael was first to respond, but before he could complain about not being consulted, say that he had too much work on, or otherwise obstruct the idea, Julie-Anne caught his eye and said, 'Yes, but I did say it would be a surprise, and it's going to be.'

'So what's the surprise?' asked Jason.

'Come on!' Julie-Anne laughed. 'If I tell you now it won't be a surprise, will it?'

'But I won't know what to wear!' Olivia wailed.

'Don't worry about that. Jeans, trainers, T-shirt, jacket. That's all you'll need.'

'What if it rains?'

'Car park to door will be the only rain hazard,' Julie-Anne affirmed.

'We are going to the cinema!' Jason declared.

'No, we aren't,' said Julie-Anne, and went on rapidly with a grin, 'and don't think I'm going to let you keep on guessing all evening while I say no, no, no. No more guesses. It's a surprise.'

Jason persisted for some time in thinking he would be able to get Julie-Anne to give it away, while Olivia continued to come up with reasons why she couldn't, or wouldn't, join in, but was eventually cajoled. Michael was quick to jump in as soon as he and Julie-Anne were alone.

'OK,' he started, 'I saw the look and I was going to argue, but what is the grand plan and why all the secrecy?'

'I think it will work better if it's a surprise, that's all.'

'So, you're not going to tell me either?'

'No,' Julie-Anne agreed. 'It's fairer that way.'

'Equally unfair, if you ask me,' Michael said, giving up the fight.

CHAPTER 15

INSPIRATION

Friday morning passed off well enough and Julie-Anne made a point of joining a busy table at lunch to avoid a quizzing from any inquisitive colleagues about the afternoon's meeting. When the leadership team assembled after lunch, Julie-Anne began with a quick explanation.

'We did a really good job on the offsite to create a vision, something to give everyone a sense of direction and purpose. And I am not surprised that as soon as we got back to business as usual that's just what we did. We did business as usual. I think everyone has done a great job communicating the vision, our thinking behind it and how we arrived at it, but we have definitely missed a trick.'

'How so?' asked Jeff.

'We've all gone back into role, back into type and back into our usual habits,' Julie-Anne responded, 'which isn't going to change anything.'

'So, what do you propose?' Paul asked, with a bit too much challenge for Julie-Anne's liking.

'Inspiration!' she replied with some spirit. Ignoring Paul's roll of the eyes, she went straight on. 'We need to inspire people to want to join us on the journey. We can't tell them they must, or they need to. That may get compliance,' she resisted the urge to look at Paul, 'but it won't build enthusiasm, it won't get the discretionary effort, the extra mile; we have to magic that up.'

'I don't want to be negative, Julie-Anne,' Vijay's measured voice broke in, 'but I have always had a problem with this kind of thing. I'm not a very inspirational sort of person I'm afraid.'

'I understand that, Vijay,' Julie-Anne told him, 'and I am not asking for a personality transplant – we are all who we are – but we can all learn some new behaviours, and that's all inspiration is, it's a set of learned behaviours. We all think about what we are going to wear to work when we get dressed in the morning, don't we? All I am asking is that every day we think for a moment or two about how we are going to *be* when we come into work as well as how we are going to look.'

'Now that is a good point,' commented Jeff. 'I would never go into a customer meeting without thinking quite hard beforehand not just about what I was going to say, but about the impression I want to give. But coming back to the office is more like coming home, so if things haven't gone too well then I am probably going to show that.'

'Exactly,' said Julie-Anne. 'It's drains and radiators.'

'It's what?' Paul asked.

'Well we all know people who brighten up a meeting when they come into the room, or when they say something, and we've all met people at some time or another, I'm sure, who drain all energy out of a group as soon as they arrive. They are the drains, and the other people are the radiators. They radiate positive energy.'

'Oh, I like that idea,' put in Naomi. 'I hope I'm a radiator. I mean, I think I do try to do that, but it probably slips a bit around month-end when there's a lot of pressure on.'

'That is an interesting idea,' Vijay added. 'I read a book a while ago about leadership in the Royal Navy. They commissioned some chap to look at the way they did things and the book was basically his report. One of the things he commented on was that

Navy Commanders all seemed to have a quality he called "learned cheerfulness".'

'Learned cheerfulness. I like that!' Jeff rubbed his hands together. 'That's going straight into the next sales meeting. Along with drains and radiators. We are supposed to have a no-whinging policy, but if you sat in when things are not going so well, you would never believe it.'

'I still think you are asking people, us specifically, to act out of character,' complained Paul.

'Not really,' Julie-Anne came back, 'we all know how to be bright and upbeat. Usually we do it when we are talking about something that we are very enthusiastic about, or when we are telling a story to an eager audience. And although I haven't read the book Vijay was talking about, I think that is saying that those leaders have learned to be bright and enthusiastic, even when things are not going well, and perhaps when they don't even feel that way themselves.'

'That's it exactly,' Vijay confirmed.

'So, we are all supposed to be actors now?' Paul seemed to be settling into a truculent mood, which was a worrying, if not altogether unexpected, development.

'Well, we talk about being in a leadership role, don't we?' Julie-Anne responded with a smile, and quickly carried on before Paul could come back on that. 'And no, we all need to be ourselves, but we need to be our best selves if we are going to be inspirational.'

'I remember being on a programme some years ago,' Naomi grinned, 'and being exhorted to bring our whole selves to work. I thought at the time that wasn't a good idea.'

'You mean we've never seen the real you?' joked Jeff.

'That's right. You have never seen truly angry me, or sulky me, or quite a few other versions of me you wouldn't want to know.'

'But you are still authentically you at work?' Julie-Anne checked in.

'Well I certainly hope so!' responded Naomi.

'So that's it,' Julie-Anne confirmed. 'We have a role model for being yourself with forethought. Bringing out the best in yourself so that you can bring out the best in others. And that's another important point. Our vision is there to give everyone a sense of purpose, the feeling that they are here to do something more than just a job, that we are all combining to do something good and useful in the world. But that won't work if we go round telling people what to do, looking over their shoulders and micromanaging them.'

'Surely none of us is behaving like that?' Vijay seemed genuinely hurt at the suggestion.

'Well I hope not,' Julie-Anne said, 'and I don't think anybody is doing that, but I do want us all to be looking positively for what people can do, what they are good at, and where they could learn new skills or expand the range of what they can do and what they know.'

'As if everyone isn't doing enough already,' muttered Paul, quickly covering himself with: 'I mean, I don't know how people feel about workloads, but surely if people have spare capacity then we have too many heads in the business?'

'No, I don't agree with that,' John came in on Julie-Anne's side. 'I think even in a business that is running relatively lean, individual people will still be able to, and indeed will want to, learn new things. It's natural. Repetition eventually becomes boring. Besides, look at the number of people using their spare time to learn a language, to learn to dance or to play music, all sorts of things. Learning is a natural human function.' Paul shrugged his shoulders but said nothing.

'We need to build confidence, be proud and model the behaviours and attitudes we want to see,' Julie-Anne declared firmly.

'Tell us a bit more about that,' said John.

'Well, leading means we go first,' Julie-Anne responded, 'so we need to be decisive, not making snap decisions, but definitely not putting off difficult decisions or delaying things. We need to be able to justify our stand on things, and we need to face up to difficult issues and have the courage to resolve them.' She paused and took a breath. 'Then we need to think about how to build everyone else's confidence. Not just in the business, but in their team, and in themselves. It's about building hope and optimism, getting everyone excited and enthusiastic about the possibilities, and we do that by demonstrating our own belief and high expectations for success. It's all about the language we use and the sentiments we share.'

Julie-Anne looked around the table. Heads were nodding, expressions looked thoughtful.

'You know, I think you're right,' Naomi said. 'Now you have described it, I realise I don't actually do very much of that. I mean I think I'm OK at the decision making. We haven't had many difficult issues, but I have, I think, been quick to step in when we have. It's more that bit about building other people's confidence. Hadn't really occurred to me if I'm honest.'

'I actually think I'm a bit the other way around,' Jeff joined in. 'I'm used to having to build people up, make them believe they can do it, that the products are great, the business is great, and all that. But I do tend to procrastinate difficult decisions. I am a big fan of masterly inactivity,' he laughed at his own joke, 'but perhaps that's not always a good thing, and I probably need to be clearer about what I expect sometimes.'

'You said something about being proud as well,' Paul remarked. 'Doesn't pride come before a fall?'

'I think that should be hubris,' Naomi said quickly. 'Excessive pride.'

'I know what hubris is,' Paul snapped back.

'Well I don't think simply being proud of what we do is going to trip us up.'

'That's just it,' Julie-Anne continued. 'Our vision is about where we are going, or what we are trying to build here, and we should be proud of that. People expect leaders to be proud of what they are trying to do, and of what they are achieving.'

'So, we ought to big-up all the things that are going well?' John asked.

'Absolutely,' Julie-Anne confirmed. 'Don't overegg it, but yes, we need to put much more effort into letting people know what is going well.'

'It's a good point,' Jeff agreed. 'Targets met: well done. Targets missed: big inquest. Perhaps we should do a bit more on the "well done" side...' he tailed off, then flipped open his small notebook and wrote rapidly for a moment.

'And lastly,' Julie-Anne confirmed, 'we all need to go out there and role model all of this. We need to set an example by behaving in ways that are consistent with our values, and we need to celebrate even the small wins that show we are on the way.'

'I'm up for it!' Jeff grinned, shutting his notebook with a snap.

'Absolutely,' agreed Naomi.

'Well of course,' added John, and finally Vijay said firmly: 'I will give it my best shot, with my best self,' he added as an afterthought. 'Although I do feel as though I am making a Boy Scout promise.'

'Nothing wrong with that, Vijay,' laughed Jeff. 'We can always get you a staff and a woggle.'

'Paul?' asked Julie-Anne.

Any discomfort Paul might have felt he chose to disguise.

'Well of course I am here to make sure everyone behaves properly in the first place and sticks to the rules. I don't see that the rest of this has very much to do with me.'

'I know your role is a little different, Paul, but you are a member of the leadership team and you do have a presence here,' Julie-Anne said calmly. 'Let's talk about it next week.'

Paul nodded, and with a little chit-chat and some good-natured banter, the meeting came to an end. As she walked to the car park, Julie-Anne's mind strayed to tomorrow and the 'family offsite', but as she belted up in her car and drove out of the car park, her thoughts returned to Paul.

'There is a difficult situation I am going to have to face up to,' she thought, 'before he brings everyone crashing back down.' But that, she decided, could most definitely wait until next week.

CHAPTER 16

THE GREAT ESCAPE

Friday evening threatened to be a repeat of Thursday, with Jason attempting to wheedle out information about the next day's activity and Olivia on the verge of a sulk about being forced into 'some stupid thing with her stupid brother' (she stopped short of 'her stupid parents'), and that she 'shouldn't have to go along with such stupid things.'

Michael, at the end of a better work week than he had anticipated, stayed calm and quietly took Julie-Anne's side. Eventually when they were alone, supper having passed off without serious incident, he asked: 'Still not telling?' and in response to Julie-Anne's grin and quick shake of her head he shrugged his shoulders and gave up on that line of enquiry.

On Saturday morning, Jason was up, dressed and down to breakfast early, still full of questions and with obvious excitement, even if he was trying not to show it too much. Olivia was late, had to be called several times, and was in a bad mood when she finally appeared. Nevertheless, everyone was in the car and ready to go on time. Julie-Anne tapped a postcode into the sat nav, tapped 'Go' on the screen and said to Michael: 'There you are, off we go.' Michael shook his head, grinned and set off.

Thirty minutes later, Michael followed the sat nav's instruction to turn left.

'Are you sure about this?' he asked Julie-Anne as they drove past a warehouse and some industrial-looking units.

'In one thousand feet you will reach your destination on your left,' the sat nav told them.

'I don't think so!' Michael chanted with a note of triumph in his voice.

'We'll see,' replied Julie-Anne as they drove past a car wash.

Around the next corner stood a single-storey building, which looked as if it had once been a small office block, attached to a larger building behind. In front of it a large sign read: No Escape – unless you're clever!

'This is the place,' Julie-Anne declared.

'OK, I've got it,' Michael said.

'What?' asked Jason.

'What we are here to do.'

'But what's that?'

'To escape! We are here to escape.'

'We could do that by just driving home again,' was Olivia's contribution.

'Now, now,' Michael admonished her. 'Let's not have an attitude problem before we have even tried this. Whatever it is.'

What it proved to be, once they had registered with reception and been briefed, was a one-hour challenge. They were on the bridge of a ship, they were told. In reality, it was a room containing an old-fashioned ship's wheel with an ocean view provided on a screen in front. The problem was that the wheel was locked in place, physically held by a chain and padlock. In sixty minutes, they were told, the ship would hit a rocky coastline, still travelling at full speed. Freeing the wheel would enable them to steer the ship away and restore communications with the engine room so that they could slow down. All the clues needed to find the key that would unlock the wheel were in the room – and so would they be for the next hour, unless they solved the problem before then.

Immediately after the door closed, Jason began rushing around. The room was full of all sorts of nautical items, rather loosely of the same vintage as the ship's wheel itself. There were suitcases, trunks and lockers, nearly all of which Jason found to be locked. There were coils of rope, brass lamps, charts and a sextant, and Jason continued picking things up and pulling at doors until Michael called out.

'Hold on a minute Jason, let's have a think about what we are doing first. If you start moving things around that might mess everything up.'

'Good call,' Julie-Anne agreed. Let's cast our eyes around, see what we can see and then we can each say what we have noticed and where we think we should start.' Olivia rolled her eyes at the suggestion. Michael was about to say something to her when he saw a strange expression on her face. Was that a little gleam of triumph? he wondered. Two minutes later they stood in a group beside the ship's wheel.

'What does everyone think?' Julie-Anne asked.

'I think we should use that long spike thing,' Jason pointed into a corner where something a little like the shank of a harpoon was leaning against the wall. 'We should use that to force open those two big chests. We could break into them.'

'I don't think that's really how we are meant to do it,' laughed Michael. 'Otherwise they'd need new chests every time.'

'Yeah, that's just *stupid*!' Olivia told Jason, causing his face to fall even further.

'Well if we are going to solve it, we will have to do it together and name-calling isn't going to help,' Julie-Anne said sharply.

Michael thought the first clue might lie in one of the charts. Julie-Anne agreed that was possible, but she thought the first clue was more likely to be something physical.

'What do you think, Livvy?' she asked. The look Michael had noticed stole back across Olivia's face. Now she was positively grinning.

'I think you're all stupid,' she said, but this time without malice. 'Look...' she pointed up at the top of the door through which they had entered the room. Lying on top of the door frame was a very large and very obvious key. 'None of you thought to look up, did you?'

'Very clever,' Michael agreed, adding, 'I never knew that thing you do when you roll your eyes up could have a useful purpose!' He stepped forward and reached up for the key.

'Oh, *I* wanted to find the first clue,' said Jason, flipping his fingers and going on a short walk of frustration.

'There'll be plenty more,' Julie-Anne told him. 'Come on, let's find out what this key fits.'

But the key didn't seem to fit anything, it was far too large for any of the drawers or cupboards and didn't appear to have any useful purpose.

'It must do *something*,' Michael said. 'Surely it can't just be a red herring?'

Jason reached out and took the key from him, turning it round in his hands. Suddenly he grasped the two ends, one in each hand, and twisted them. The key obligingly unscrewed itself into two parts revealing a roll of paper hidden inside. Jason was beside himself with glee.

'I did it, he said, 'I found the first *proper* clue!'

Olivia started to argue but Julie-Anne intervened. 'We've got one hour, well actually now about fifty-five minutes, to get out of here; arguing will only waste time.'

The message on the roll of paper was written in some sort of code, and this time it was Michael's turn, spotting a simple substitution that made gobbledygook into plain English and led them to another clue. As the clues revealed yet more steps to take and puzzles to solve the time ticked by. Michael had started furtively checking his watch. Jason's eyes kept straying back to the harpoon shank.

'What are you thinking?' Julie-Anne asked him.

'Well, somewhere it said the last clue is like the first one but the other way around.'

'Yes?'

'The first clue was a piece of paper rolled up inside that big key.'

'That was *actually* the second clue,' Olivia broke in.

'So maybe the last clue is the key we need for the padlock, wrapped up in a roll of paper somewhere.'

'Brilliant!' exclaimed Michael, as Jason pointed to the harpoon shaft. Michael grabbed it and tapped it.

'It's hollow, like bamboo or something,' he confirmed.

'But how do we get into it?' asked Olivia.

'We could break it in half,' Jason shouted, miming the act of snapping a branch across his knee.

'I don't think so,' replied Michael, 'and in fact we don't need to. There's a cap on this end.'

At that moment, an ominous ticking started to sound. The ship's clock on the wall, which had seemed to be broken, had sprung into life and was counting down the last minute of the hour. Michael wrestled with the cap. He pulled at it, pushed it with his thumbs, and tried unscrewing it, all to no avail. With seconds to go on the clock, Olivia shouted out: 'Turn it the other way!'

The cap spun off in Michael's hand, he turned the shank, and a long roll of paper, a nautical chart, slid out. Scrabbling on hands and knees they unrolled it to find a small key. Jason grabbed it and leapt to the padlock securing the ship's wheel. One complete turn of the key and it opened. Olivia threw the chains off the wheel and the clock stopped, with just three seconds to go. For a moment no-one said anything at all, then quite spontaneously they all whooped at once.

On the return car journey, there was no more bickering, just a recounting of all the clues they had solved and close agreement between Olivia and Jason on how clever everyone had been.

Back at home, Michael confided in Julie-Anne: 'You know, I had serious doubts about that, but you seemed so convinced about the idea that I didn't want to say anything.'

'I had no idea whether it would work either,' Julie-Anne told him. 'I guess that if we hadn't unlocked the wheel then recriminations would still be going on as to whose fault that was. But as it is, we seem to have created a little bit of family harmony with our offsite.'

'Well here's to that,' said Michael, 'and long may it continue.'

CHAPTER 17

BAD NEWS

Still basking in the success of Saturday's 'family offsite', Julie-Anne felt a twinge of alarm when early on Sunday evening her phone buzzed with a message and glancing at the screen she could see it was from Ted Williams. It read: *Need to talk, apologies for weekend call but can we Zoom in 10?* Julie-Anne pulled a face and called up to Michael, who had retreated to his upstairs office.

'Ted Williams has just messaged; I need to talk to him.'

'On a Sunday?' Michael called back, 'It doesn't get any better does it? The job that never ends!' Ignoring the fact that Michael was spending his Sunday evening working, Julie-Anne shouted back.

'I'll let you know when I am off the call,' which Michael acknowledged with 'OK.'

Julie-Anne set up her laptop on the kitchen table, opened her email, found the meeting invitation from Ted with a link in it and clicked it. Ted's face appeared on the screen almost immediately. He was sitting in his den, as he referred to it – she recognised the baseball pennant on the wall behind Ted, together with some other sporting trophies and memorabilia.

'Hi, Julie-Anne!' he said enthusiastically. 'Sorry for the Sunday call, how has your weekend been?'

'Pretty good so far, thanks,' Julie-Anne replied, thinking she was not going to get into a social exchange at this point, basic pleasantries would be enough. 'How about you?'

'Well Parker hit a triple in his game on Saturday, and they won, which was great.' Julie-Anne did not know much about baseball, but she had absorbed enough of Ted's son's progress to know that a triple was good, and she acknowledged as much. Ted, wisely, got down to business.

'We are having a pretty hard time of things here,' he began. Julie-Anne waited. She knew her figures were not good, but she was not about to start justifying things until Ted had had his say. To her surprise, Ted started by focussing on his home market rather than Julie-Anne's European operation.

'Yes,' Ted carried on, 'sales are down, earnings are down. People must be getting healthier!' he joked.

'What is it really, Ted?'

'It's twofold actually. We all know that Myovilite is going off patent, but we have already had to fend off one or two generics companies from trying to muscle in early. We have had to threaten them with legal action, which seems to have worked, but not before they got quite a lot of product into the market over here. That's been factor one. Factor two is sort of the opposite of that. Some clinics seemed to think that far from a bunch of imitators coming into the market, there might be a shortage. Not sure how they worked that out, but sometimes there's no accounting for folk. Anyway, some of them stockpiled, and now they are ahead of what they need. So, all in all, it's been a rough quarter.'

'How bad?' Julie-Anne asked.

'We are about fifteen per cent down. Which is bad, but what is worse is attitudes. Everyone is walking around like the living dead. The place is zombified.'

'Really, just on one quarter's results?'

'I think it's come as a shock to a lot of people. Don't forget, people have had things very easy for quite some time. Now they've had a wake-up call. They are thinking "well, what does happen when Myovilite comes off patent?"'

'I have been wondering that myself,' Julie-Anne admitted. 'There hasn't been much information recently.'

'No, and that's what I really wanted to talk to you about. Axxanent, the replacement product has been delayed. We look like having a big gap between the end of Myovilite and Axxanent actually coming on stream.'

'Oh, that's not good.'

'Damn right it's not. The water cooler conversation round here is all about whether the Group will sell us off, or even shut us down.'

'Surely not! That wouldn't make any sense.'

'Well, you know, it might. Forecasts for Axxanent are not that great. If it's going to be late coming through while the Myovilite market is flooded with generics, now might be a good time to simply cut all this cost.'

'You mean cut all the people?'

'Well, that's always where most of the cost is, isn't it? Anyway, this is not for public consumption, I just wanted to let you know how things stand and what might be coming down the pike.'

Ted signed off, leaving Julie-Anne to ponder. How could she possibly walk into work tomorrow being a radiator of positive energy, inspiring those around her and working towards her vision, in the face of that news?

CHAPTER 18

RADIATORS AND DRAINS

Julie-Anne sat in her car for a moment after parking, her own words coming back to her from the team meeting. 'We all know how to be cheerful and upbeat,' she told herself. 'Just think about the things that motivate you and make you feel good, instead of dwelling on all the fears and worries. And if that sounds too much like a piece of sanctimonious self-help,' she added, 'have a think about which line of thought is going to make you more resourceful to deal with the problems.'

She got out of the car with a smile on her face and walked across the car park as if she was on the red carpet at a premiere. She stopped to say hello to Patti and Frank on Reception, asking each of them how their weekend had been, and then headed up the stairs. The ground floor of the building was meeting and conference rooms along with the refectory, with the offices on the floor above. Before swiping her security card to gain access, Julie-Anne paused, took a deep breath and, putting her head right back, looked straight up at the ceiling and smiled broadly. She couldn't remember where she had learned that trick but, boy did it work! The positive feeling, along with the smile, lasted all the way across the open office space, through all the quick calls of 'Hi,' and 'Good Morning,' and the bits of chit-chat, and was still with her when she sat down at her own desk.

John Harris looked in. His usual khaki chinos and tan leather brogues were topped off by an eye-catching striped shirt in red, white and yellow.

'Morning!' he called out from the doorway, and then walked in as Julie-Anne looked up. 'You look cheerful. Good news!'

'No, not really. I spoke to Ted last night, and the truth is, things are not great.'

'Well, no-one would know that from looking at you.'

'That's good to hear, I was rather aiming at that.'

'How do you mean?' asked John, sitting down.

'Well, as I see it,' Julie-Anne explained, 'a large part of my job is to take on pressure, that's the pressure that comes down from above as well the pressures here, and then help the team reach creative solutions to those pressures, and the things that are causing them. Oh, and of course to do that without denying the anxiety. We have to acknowledge things and then find positive ways of dealing with them.'

'Wow. So that's all part of this inspiration thing you were talking to us about?'

'Certainly is!'

'So, we are laughing in the face of adversity?'

'I wouldn't quite go that far, but maybe something along those lines, yes,' Julie-Anne said with a note of caution. 'We don't want everyone thinking we have lost the plot altogether,' she added with a grin.

'Hmm. So, cheerfully, what did Ted have to say?'

'The Axxanent launch is delayed and they have been hit by generic suppliers, so the quarter's figures are terrible and there's a lot of gloom and despondency about.'

'I'm surprised about the generics. I mean Myovilite is still on patent. What happened?'

'Well it's not for the first time, although it is a first for us. By the time they realised what was happening, got the lawyers involved and all of that, a lot of product had already got out. Everyone was then told that they couldn't use it, and by the time all that happened, a lot of it had been used. No danger to patients of course, it is all correctly formulated by known generics companies; there is no problem with their product.'

'Just their business ethics.'

'Well yes, but the important thing is not what's happened but what we are going to do about it over here.'

'And what are we going to do about it?'

'I've been thinking about that. Ted was saying that he thought people had had it easy for a long time. That's not to be critical, but when success comes easily you don't have to change much and people soon become resistant to learning new things.'

'Oh, so you think we all need to be developing some new skills, to go along with our new ways of behaving?'

'I do,' Julie-Anne told him. 'I definitely do.'

CHAPTER 19

BATTLE ON THE HOME FRONT

Walking back into the house that evening, Julie-Anne began to wonder whether she would be needing to develop some new parenting skills. The atmosphere of 'we can solve things together as a family' seemed to have evaporated and been replaced by gloom and anger.

On being asked how she was, Olivia burst into tears and ran upstairs to her room. Turning to Jason to ask what was wrong resulted only in him shouting: 'It's not just Olivia! I'll be without Johnny as well!' and making a similarly rapid exit. Shaking her head, Julie-Anne put down her bag and sat down as Michael entered the room.

'What on Earth is going on?'

'Oh, you're lucky,' he replied. 'That, or something very like it, has been going on since they both got in from school.'

'And…?'

Michael sat down with a sigh. 'Beverley's father has taken a job in America. The whole family is moving to New York – Bob, Margaret and the children…'

'Oh, my word, so Beverley's leaving?'

'That's it.'

'And that's why Jason is joining in. He does do quite a lot with Beverley's brother, doesn't he?'

Beverley was Olivia's best friend. Julie-Anne knew it must have hit her daughter hard.

'Poor Olivia,' said Julie-Anne thoughtfully. 'They are so close. That must be almost like a bereavement.'

'Well don't make it worse than it is,' protested Michael, 'they can skype, or text, that's what they spend most of their lives doing anyway.'

'Except they also see each other every day of term time and a lot of the time in the holidays as well. It's not the same.'

'I didn't say it was, but I've been trying to explain to Olivia that it's not actually the end of the world, and now you're talking about people dying!' Michael threw up his hands.

'OK, OK, let's both hold on a moment.' Julie-Anne took a breath and continued more calmly. 'I understand you have had to deal with a lot of emotions since they came in, but this will be a real upheaval for Olivia. It's a major change and most of us don't respond very well to change, especially when it comes as a big shock.'

'Honestly, you'd think the world had ended!'

'Well for Olivia a little bit of it probably just has.'

'So, what do you suggest?' Michael asked, his voice rising.

'I'm not sure, but one thing I do know is that an inspirational speech is certainly not going to do it.'

'I have been trying to explain to Olivia that things happen in life which are not what any of us would choose,' said Michael, sounding dangerously tetchy, 'and that all she can do is stay in touch with Beverley and deal with it. I mean they text each other all day long anyway. I can't see that it's so very different.'

'Well, that certainly wasn't an inspirational speech,' Julie-Anne pursed her lips into a wry smile. 'How did that go down?'

'Like the proverbial lead balloon. "I don't understand, I'm hateful, she hates me, I must hate her to even think something like that let alone say it…" shall I go on?'

'No, no, I've got the picture thanks.'

'So, for the second time of asking, what do you suggest?'

'Let's try a little empathy. What was the worst thing that happened to you growing up?'

Michael thought for a minute. 'I was going to say being dumped by Katya McLoughlin, but on balance it was probably when Robbie died.'

'Your first dog?'

'Yes, he was getting older but seemed perfectly normal. One day someone rang the doorbell, he went to the front door and barked, and by the time I got there he was slumped against the wall, then he just kind of slithered onto the floor.' Julie-Anne knew the story, but she let Michael tell it. 'We got him to the vet, and they asked us to leave him there. They called back later that day. It was cancer, and it had spread all through him. They said the kindest thing would be to end it for him then and there. I agreed but I asked to see him, then the vet said that wasn't a good idea. They had had to open him up, so his belly was all shaved, he'd be full of stitches. I took their advice to remember him as he was. I still do actually.' Michael flicked the corner of one eye with the knuckle of his first finger. Julie-Anne waited a moment before speaking.

'So, that was tough?'

'Yes, it was,' Michael nodded.

'So, Olivia is having a tough time. Maybe we should acknowledge that and try to help her come out of it a bit stronger.'

'How do you mean?'

'Well our job is to help Olivia and Jason grow up, isn't it? And growing up means developing some resilience and maybe a little bit of... emotional maturity, perhaps?'

'Sounds a bit New Age to me.'

'Well it might not be the best choice of words, but you get the idea.'

'I see where you are going,' Michael said. 'What do you suggest we do?'

Julie-Anne thought about that for a moment before replying. 'Approach with caution and try to help Olivia see that while friendships are great, important and necessary, independence is valuable too.'

CHAPTER 20

CHANGING HABITS

The weekly leadership team meeting did not start well. Intentions were good, but there was a sense of bad news hovering even before Julie-Anne invited Naomi to start the 'lightning round', which involved everyone giving a one-minute update on their area and any immediate challenges. The outputs of that round formed the agenda for the rest of the meeting, with time allocated to each item. At the end of the lightning round, Julie-Anne checked the items she had noted with everyone and turned to Jeff.

'Let's start with your challenge, Jeff. Customer Relationship Management?'

'OK, yes,' Jeff launched in with enthusiasm. 'CRM. It's not the customer relationships that are the problem. As you know the point of a CRM system is to have all the information about any given customer account in one place. However, it's like any other computer system, what you can see depends on what's been put into it. The challenge is getting our salespeople to use it properly. As you know, most of our people have been in role for a long time, they have years of experience and a lot of expertise.' He paused for a moment and smiled as he added: 'They really are very good, you know!'

'They just don't want to do what you are asking them to,' put in Paul, rather too sharply for Julie-Anne's liking. She was about to say something, but Jeff took it in his stride.

'If you like, yes. That's about the size of it,' Jeff agreed with a shrug. 'And yes, before you ask, I am concerned that if I start to come down too hard about it some of them may simply up sticks and head off to pastures new.'

'So, it's not really about the system then?' John asked. 'It's really about behaviour change?'

'Absolutely,' Jeff replied. 'The system is a bit clunky to be honest, it's not the slickest thing in the world but it's really no different to any other piece of admin.'

'Like filling in an expense claim?' asked Paul. 'I bet everyone's quick enough to do that!'

'You know, that's a really good point,' Jeff acknowledged. 'And I could actually use that one of two ways.'

'Go on,' Vijay chipped in.

'Well, I could make the point that everyone does indeed fill in their expenses, in detail and accurately, on an automated system, because they know that if they don't, they won't get them paid without a lot of queries. Therefore, it's not a skill or training issue. I could make that point, which is a positive one.'

'And, on the other hand?' Vijay was smiling.

'I know where you are coming from,' Jeff went on. 'I could threaten that if the CRM system is not bang up to date for all accounts they are responsible for, then they won't get their expenses, at least until such time that it is up to date.'

'I thought you didn't want to be heavy-handed,' Paul complained.

'No,' Jeff grinned, 'but behaviour change generally depends on consequences. So perhaps if I stress the benefits, of which there are many, and appeal to people's professionalism and make a veiled reference to compliance,' here Paul snorted loudly, 'that might just do it. OK, that's me done, I'll report back next week. Who's next?'

'Well, funnily enough,' Naomi came in quickly, 'I have a similar issue, but it only concerns one person. As you know, we are migrating the financial software onto a new system and generally people are coping very well with the change, but Humaira is really struggling with it.'

'Do you know why?' Julie-Anne asked.

'No, not really. I'm trying to be helpful because she is very good and, like Jeff with his team, I don't want to lose her. She seems extremely stressed by the whole changeover, but I'm not quite sure why.'

'She's been here a long time, hasn't she?' Vijay said thoughtfully.

'Longer than me,' Naomi admitted.

'Set in her ways,' Paul interjected in a sharp tone of voice.

'I was thinking something else,' Vijay replied. 'Humaira has always struck me as being extremely conscientious. Something I would think would appeal to you, Paul,' he added. Paul said nothing. 'I think that perhaps Humaira is very proud of what she does and is afraid that in trying to learn the new system she will make mistakes. She might fail to meet her own high standards, and that would be very upsetting for her.'

'Well,' Naomi responded after a pause. 'I certainly hadn't thought about that, but the more I do think about it, the more I think you might be right.'

'It does sound very likely, but we ought not just to conclude that Vijay is right. It could be something else entirely,' John put in.

'It might very well be,' Vijay agreed. 'How about getting her a coach? Someone who might be able to help her through it without imposing a solution.'

Naomi nodded thoughtfully and glanced at Julie-Anne.

'Fine by me,' Julie-Anne said, 'good idea.'

The rest of the meeting passed quickly. John described a technical problem about labelling but declared that it was only to keep everyone informed, he had a solution in progress. Vijay had no issues and Paul simply shook his head when asked.

'Well that just leaves me,' Julie-Anne noted. 'And here's my issue. I think we are trying to get the whole organisation to change, and we haven't thought about the development we need to do to make sure it happens.'

'How do you mean?' asked Jeff.

'Well, we are asking people to learn new systems, new ways of working, new products, and we are assuming those are the changes we need to make. We are committed to being radiators, not drains, and we want other people to be like that too. However, what we are talking about is a lot more than simply learning how to use a different system. We are talking about personal development, we are talking about people having a growth mindset, about being positive and open to new possibilities. That's the real change we need to make. We need to develop our people so that *they* are the business we need to become.'

'Interesting thought,' John said after a collective pause for breath. 'I see what you mean as well. We are busy trying to transform the business, expecting everyone to go along with the changes, but actually if we are going to become a different business then we need different people.'

'Are you suggesting mass redundancies?' Paul jumped in.

'No of course not,' retorted John. 'I'm with Julie-Anne though. Think about what you have to do to turn a losing team into a winning one.'

'Who said we are losing?' interjected Jeff.

'It's just an analogy,' John replied. 'Take a sports team, you might have to raise levels of fitness, have people learn new skills, get better at old ones, all of that. But you have also got to inject a winning mentality, you must change people's outlook, and to do that you'll need to change some behaviours.'

'So how would we do that?' asked Naomi.

'We'll need to start by changing ourselves.' The quiet voice was Vijay's. 'We'll need to set the example. After all, leading means you go first.'

'How do you mean?' asked John.

'Well I think firstly we should check in on the skills training,' Vijay replied. 'Perhaps we could get some of the Finance team to show Sales how their new software works, and Sales could return the favour by demonstrating the CRM system, and we should make it clear that we are offering more training if it is using either of the systems that is a problem. But as far as starting with ourselves, perhaps we need to demonstrate some personal change.'

'In that case I have a challenge for you all,' Julie-Anne announced. 'Try changing everything. Change the way you dress, your route to work. Eat something different, read a different paper or magazine, listen to some different music...' she paused and smiled at the bemused faces looking back at her.

'It works, believe me. If you really want to change things, try shaking up *all* the things you do habitually.'

Jeff was first to react with a sudden laugh. 'Sounds weird. I might just try it!' he exclaimed.

'I like that too,' agreed Naomi. Vijay pulled a face and, having started to declare that he was too old a dog to start learning new tricks, backtracked and said he might try changing some things, just to see what happened. John too was cautious but not dismissive.

Paul said: 'Well I'll be leaving things as they are.'

CHAPTER 21

DEVELOPMENT

'Good day?' Michael asked.

'Not bad. Quite interesting in fact.'

'How so?'

'I realised that we are trying to change a lot of things but that we have been neglecting the development piece.'

'I'm not with you.'

'Learning. New skills, different ways of doing things, developing potential.'

'Doesn't all that just annoy most people? I mean, time away from the day job, being sent off on training courses and so on?'

Julie-Anne thought about that for a minute. 'You know, you might be right there – but only if it's done badly. Most people like learning new things.'

'Well that's not been my recent experience asking Livvy and Jason about school.'

'Sort of proves my point, I think,' Julie-Anne responded. 'They are being made to learn things that aren't their choice. They may be very valuable things...'

'Or not,' Michael put in. 'Ask most people how much of their school education they have ever used since!'

'My point exactly! Yet every time I hear you playing your guitar you are trying to learn something new rather than playing something you already know how to play. Which can be very frustrating to listen to, but leaving that on one side,' Julie-Anne forestalled any conversation about guitar practice, 'what I wonder is, what would they really like to be learning?'

'Well, for Jason that would be whatever the next gaming craze is after Minecraft and Fortnite, and for Olivia it's probably how to stop your best friend moving away with her family.'

'A cynic is a passionate person who doesn't want to be disappointed again,' Julie-Anne reminded him – she had used the phrase before.

'Are you saying I am disappointed?' retorted Michael.

'No, passionate,' Julie-Anne told him. 'We both are, aren't we? We want the best for our children, and do you know, as well as that, I want the best for all the people in the business.'

'Meaning?'

'Meaning I am going to find out what Olivia and Jason would really like to learn about, and what people in my business want to be learning. I think that might be quite motivating all round!'

'I'll tell you what,' Michael said after a moment's reflection, 'why don't you let me ask Olivia and Jason about that, and you can focus on what you need to be doing at work?'

Julie-Anne took a deep breath, reflected on her view that teamwork starts in trust, and said: 'OK – and thank you. I do have quite a lot going on in the business right now.'

CHAPTER 22

LISTENING IN

Julie-Anne had never been one to hide behind a closed door, even when she had an office of her own, so no-one was surprised to see her walking the floor. If anyone was surprised to be asked a few questions about how they were feeling no-one showed it. Each time, Julie-Anne artfully brought the conversation round to the subject of learning. What did people really want to learn or to find out about?

Some of the answers surprised her, but like the good consultant she had set out to be, she noted all the answers, including the off-the-cuff responses, the ones seemingly nothing to do with work, and the flippant and the funny.

Towards the end of the morning, she bumped into John Harris on his way back from a meeting.

'You've caused a bit of a stir this morning!' he said brightly. 'I'm just wondering though, aren't you in danger of creating expectations that won't be met? I mean just because someone wants to learn German or play the ukulele doesn't mean we are going to start sending them off on courses.' He paused and then asked: 'Does it?' in a rather less certain tone.

Julie-Anne laughed. 'No, that's not the idea at all,' she told him. 'Although I do have an idea, which is more than I did when I started this morning.' John cocked his head to one side and raised an eyebrow.

'No, I am going to hold onto that one for now but let me tell you what gave me the idea.' John waited until Julie-Anne went on. 'The answer that came up most often, not just about what people want to learn, but about what would help them do their job better, is to find out what other people do!'

'*Really?*' John looked as astonished as he sounded.

'Yes, really,' Julie-Anne confirmed. 'And there is a very simple solution to that one.'

'Which is?'

'We get people to show each other. It doesn't have to be a full-on job swap, but if we arrange a programme where people spend time at each other's desks, in different departments, to understand other people's jobs and how everyone contributes, that could help bridge a few silos.'

'Do we have silos?'

'Not exactly, I think it's more that people just have their heads down. But you know as well as I do that when everyone is focussed on their own small world and the pressure intensifies, the barriers start to go up. It's a natural defence against feeling overwhelmed.'

'There's something in that, certainly,' John agreed. 'And if people really want to do what you are suggesting, it shouldn't be too hard to organise. What's your plan for all the other things though, you said you had a bright idea?'

'Oh yes, we should start a marketplace. Let people advertise either something they can teach or something they would like to learn. Then those who want to can get together, point people towards useful resources, or explain how they learned to do something. To be honest we could start it using a simple pinboard.'

'Yes, although it shouldn't be too difficult to get something up on the intranet if it's only for us. I'll have a word with IT and see what might be possible.'

CHAPTER 23

JUST ONE MORE THING

Two days later, Naomi stopped by Julie-Anne's office.

'I just came to say that your cross-learning initiative has gone down very well with my team,' Naomi said, taking the visitor's chair and putting her coffee cup down. Julie-Anne checked her screen one more time and hit 'send' on a long email to Ted Williams. The time difference meant she would probably be waiting a while for a reply.

'That's really good news,' she told Naomi.

'Actually, it's even better than that.'

'How so?'

'I think there is a real energy about the place this last week. This feeling that everyone is learning seems to be very uplifting. People are sounding a lot more positive. I must say I think the vision has done a lot in that respect as well. It's reminded people of what we are here for, and I do think that had got a bit lost. As far as my team goes, I'm trying to be a bit more hands off as well. I mean you can't really be inspirational while standing over people and telling them what to do, can you?'

Julie-Anne laughed. 'I had never really thought about it like that, but no, you can't!'

'This whole learning idea has really got people enthused,' Naomi went on. 'It seems to have touched a chord.'

'Shall I tell you how I realised that? I started to listen to people talking about what they had done at the weekend. Most people seem to be quite energised talking about things they obviously enjoyed doing at the weekend, which probably wouldn't be the case if they were describing yesterday at work. What really struck me though was the number of times people were describing getting better at something. Not just family time, or going to the cinema, eating out. All of those featured, but I heard people talking about cycling further, faster or up more hills, same with running. We have quite a few Parkrun regulars. None of them are aiming at the National Cross-country Championships, but they all compare times, and most of all they compare their latest time with their best time. They are racing against themselves. It's the same with John and Vijay they both play golf – and they are always talking about how to improve their games, whether it's their clubs, their swing or something to do with putting.

'I've never understood the attraction of golf,' Naomi laughed.

'Me neither, but I do get that it's probably the perfect game for playing against yourself – trying every time to do it better.'

'Hence the learning idea?'

'Yes, absolutely. It's funny, isn't it? People generally don't like change, but most of us do like learning.'

'So, let me see if I have understood this,' Naomi said. 'By creating a vision, we have given people a sense of why we are here, what we are all here for,' she paused, 'a sense of purpose if you like.' Julie-Anne nodded in agreement as Naomi continued, 'All of us starting to use some of these inspirational behaviours sets the tone, creates a culture of confidence, a sense of belief if you like, that we can and will deliver.' Julie-Anne was smiling broadly now as well as nodding. 'And this third piece, all about getting everyone learning, not only builds skills but also motivates people at the same time.'

'Do you know,' Julie-Anne told her, 'I had never really thought it through exactly like that, or at least not so succinctly, but that's it in a nutshell. I'm no theorist – I just know that this stuff works, or rather has worked everywhere I have seen it put into action. Which reminds me, there is a fourth thing we need to do.'

'And that is?'

Julie-Anne paused before saying. 'Let me talk to everyone at once about that – at the next leadership team meeting.'

'OK,' Naomi responded slowly, 'very mysterious. Personally, I can't wait to find out.'

CHAPTER 24

CRISIS

The next leadership team meeting began as a more sombre affair than Julie-Anne had imagined. It also started with Ted Williams calling in on speakerphone.

'I know this is unusual,' Ted began. 'It's pretty unusual for me too, but I wanted to speak to all of you at once rather than just to Julie-Anne and then leave her to pass on the news.' He paused. 'Which is that there is a very real risk Imaging may be closed down.' He paused long enough for John to say: 'What?' very loudly, while everyone else around the table exchanged looks of concern and dismay.

'I know, I know,' Ted went on. 'It's by no means certain, and it's most definitely not public information. The official line, which will be published in the next hour or so, is that the business is looking for offers for Imaging, seeking a buyer, or something like that. But the inside line is that if no-one wants us then closure is likely.'

'Ted,' it was Vijay who spoke, instinctively leaning closer to the speakerphone in the middle of the table. 'I appreciate you telling us this personally, and in confidence ahead of us finding out some other way, but what exactly are we supposed to do in the face of this news?'

'Officially, nothing. I am about to go into a meeting with my team over here and we are going to try and figure out what we can possibly do to make the best of the situation.'

'And we will do the same over here, Ted,' Julie-Anne told him, and with some hasty calls of goodbye, the teleconference was over.

'Well,' remarked Jeff. 'Bit of a bombshell! Should we end the meeting now and all go off and get our CVs up to date?'

'When the going gets tough…' Naomi said, leaving the rest of the sentence hanging in the air.

'Good point,' rejoined Jeff, 'but exactly where should we get going?'

'It's probably not "where", but "what".' Vijay chipped in. 'What should we get going on?'

'OK,' said Julie-Anne. 'Let's all take a few minutes to gather our thoughts, then we'll go round the table one at a time and find out what everyone thinks.'

With a few murmurs of assent, everyone reached for a pen and pad, save for Paul, who sat, lips pursed, staring into the middle distance. Julie-Anne glanced at him but said nothing and got on with making her own notes.

After a few minutes, pens stopped moving and people started to look up around the table and sit back. Paul, doing completely the opposite, reached for a sheet of paper and wrote six short notes in neat, rapid handwriting.

'Everyone ready?' Julie-Anne asked. 'OK, let's do it like this. I'd like everyone to take notes on what everyone else says, and to do it on one sheet of paper, like this.' She held up her pad, open to a fresh page on which she had drawn a vertical line down the middle and two horizontal ones, dividing the page into six rectangles. With some shrugs and amused looks everyone complied.

'Here's how it goes,' Julie-Anne went on. 'I am going to nominate someone to facilitate the first round. The facilitator's job is to ask someone, anyone, for their thoughts. That person then uses their own notes to say what they think, and the facilitator's job is to disallow any interruptions. When the speaker has finished, the facilitator asks whether there are any questions for clarification – and disallows anything that is a challenge, a different opinion or starting to debate a point. Once we have had any clarifications, the facilitator will ask someone else to summarise what's been said.' At this point, Jeff laughed.

'Now I see the point of this note-taking lark. Still not sure about the one piece of paper though.'

'We'll come to that a bit later,' Julie-Anne told him, adding, 'Jeff, why don't you facilitate the first round?'

'OK,' Jeff looked around the table with a grin. 'Let's hear your thoughts, Vijay.' Nobody tried to interrupt as Vijay detailed his thinking. Everyone was listening hard and jotting down Vijay's points as he elaborated them one by one. When Vijay had finished, Jeff looked around and, relishing his role to a degree, asked: 'Are there any questions for clarification?'

Naomi asked Vijay to expand on something but rapidly started to nod.

'Ah, got it, thanks!' she said.

Paul started to say something, then stopped abruptly.

'Paul?' asked Jeff.

With a rare flash of a smile, Paul responded, saying: 'No. I was about to say something when I realised it wouldn't qualify as a clarification. Interesting.'

'Well why don't you sum up for us what Vijay has said?' Jeff asked.

'Yes, of course,' Paul replied, and proceeded to summarise Vijay's points very neatly, without repeating them word for word.

'Vijay?' Jeff asked when Paul had finished.

'Very good,' said Vijay. 'Absolutely.' Paul nodded an acknowledgement.

Jeff looked across at Julie-Anne. 'What happens now?' he asked.

'Oh, you nominate the next facilitator,' she told him.

'Oh, right. Well in that case, Naomi, would you be our next facilitator please?'

'I'll be delighted,' Naomi replied with a smile.

After forty minutes, everyone had played the facilitator's role, everyone had spoken and everyone had summarised someone else's thoughts.

'Now,' Julie-Anne explained, 'you can use the sixth box on your notes page for a summary of your own points, and then we all have everyone's thinking in front of us on one piece of paper.'

'Ah, I *see!*' exclaimed Jeff.

'Yes, that's really very clever,' Paul commented, to Julie-Anne's surprise.

'What we can do now,' she announced, 'is look for linkages and commonalities. Obviously we may have some "snaps" where two people have said the same thing, and that's worth noting, but really what we are looking for is things that we can link together to form bigger ideas or more powerful concepts. Oh, and when you have found one, see if you can give it a name.'

'I'm not really sure if this counts,' said Vijay after a few minutes, 'but there is a very strong thread about the fact that we can't change the product and that Axxanent won't be along in a hurry. If you combine that with Paul's comment that US sales are a lot bigger than Europe, it is hard to see what we can do to affect things very much. Sorry if that's a bit negative.'

'Well at least it shows alignment on something,' commented Paul.

'There is a very strong theme about the people and the potential we have though,' said Naomi. 'Both in this team and in the business as a whole, and I think that links up with Jeff's comment about professional integrity and Paul's one about standards. I'm not sure what to call it though.'

'How about People and Potential?' asked Julie-Anne, 'that's what you just said.'

'Yes, but I don't want to lose the "professional" bit,' said Jeff, 'that's very important to me.'

'Professional People and Potential?' suggested Julie-Anne, to general agreement.

Gradually two main lines of thought emerged, seemingly opposed to one another. The first set of linkages was all about the quality of people and relationships in the business, the second, more threateningly, concerned the market, the products and the US business. All these factors seemed to be beyond immediate solutions and gradually the mood became more sombre again.

'Makes a bit of a mockery of our hard-won vision, doesn't it?' remarked Jeff after a long silence.

'Yes, I'm afraid it does rather,' agreed Vijay. 'It's hard to see how to have a very positive vision under the circumstances though.'

Paul looked around the table with a thin smile and shrugged his shoulders as if to say I told you so.

'Well I don't agree,' Naomi cut in. 'We may not have the answers to all our problems, but what we have done is to identify a lot of very powerful resources, and we can put those to work so that if there is a solution we will find it.

'And if there isn't?' asked Paul.

'Then we'll make sure we preside over the most professional sale or shut down of a business there has ever been!' said Jeff with sudden enthusiasm.'

'That's great,' Naomi came back, 'and then we'll have a party for everyone in the office to celebrate what we have achieved together.'

'Then we'll tidy up and leave the whole place looking immaculate,' added Vijay.

'And we'll turn the lights out when we leave,' Julie-Anne put in, 'but only if we're forced to!'

CHAPTER 25

PAST, PRESENT AND FUTURE

'I see, so how are you going to announce that?' Michael asked once Julie-Anne had explained to him how the team meeting had ended. 'Doesn't sound exactly like an inspirational message to me.' He was standing at the kitchen island slicing aubergines lengthways on a board.

'I've been thinking about that,' Julie-Anne said. 'It is going to be a Town Hall meeting, you know, with everybody there, but I'm not sure yet what I am going to say. If I asked you to name a highly inspirational speech made in hard times, what would you go for?'

Michael paused slicing for a moment then grinned and said: 'Martin Luther King – I have a dream.'

'Great choice,' responded Julie-Anne. 'How does it start?'

'Umm. I'm embarrassed to say that "I have a dream"; is the only bit I remember. No, wait, there's that bit about his children being judged not by the colour of their skin but by the content of their character. I've always loved that phrase.'

'It's a wonderful use of words, isn't it?' Julie-Anne agreed, 'but at that point he's talking about the country and the society he wants to see in the future. He *starts* by talking about the Emancipation Agreement. He starts with 'Five score years ago.' That's in the past.'

'OK, so…'

'Then he talks about the present, about all the challenges, the inequalities and the racism that people were suffering at the time. *Then* he gets to "I have a dream".'

'So, you're saying there is a formula there, an underlying structure?'

'Yes, exactly. Past, present, future. That's what I am going to talk about in the morning. Where we have come from and everything we have achieved. Where we are now, and I'm going to remain very positive about the present.'

'And what are you going to say about the future?' Michael turned up the heat under a large pan and poured oil into it.

'Well I'm not going to say everything will be all right, because I don't know that it will be. I'm not about to turn into Pollyanna. What I am going to say is that if there is a way for the business to carry on and continue to be successful then I am confident that together we will find it.'

'That level of conviction should certainly help to build confidence. You won't do that without being clear about what you believe and what you think might be possible.'

'Exactly,' responded Julie-Anne.

'You seem to have had some success inspiring your children as well,' Michael said with a smile.

'Really?' Julie-Anne was startled. 'How come?'

'That idea you had about finding out what they might like to learn.' Michael turned back to the board and began chopping large tomatoes into chunks.

'Well, come on,' Julie-Anne said. 'Don't string it out!'

'OK. Well I did rather creep up on it with each of them, but Olivia wants to go ice skating.'

'That must be the *Dancing on Ice* effect. Finally, watching television leads to something useful. And Jason?'

97

'Coding classes. Saturday afternoons, so he can still do sport in the morning if he wants to.'

'You win this week's parenting prize, that's for sure. And do I detect Pasta alla Norma in the making over there?'

'You do indeed.' Michael swept the thinly sliced aubergine into the pan and sprinkled dried oregano over the top.

'Olivia's favourite.'

'Exactly, and Jason likes it too. We are finally about to have that family pasta meal. Now I realise that as soon as we have eaten you are going to disappear into a laptop and start working out what you are going to say tomorrow, so while I carry on cooking tell me a bit more about what you plan to say.'

'Well it won't just be me. I'll be doing the talking, but the team have agreed that everyone will be there standing shoulder to shoulder, so that we are all seen to be one hundred per cent behind the message.'

'Including Paul Nettleton?'

'Including Paul. He hasn't really declared it, but he has definitely come round a bit. I think that secretly he is finding it more rewarding to be a part of the team than to sit outside it and snipe.'

'Well that would be a victory. What's brought that about?'

'I think it's partly that he came in expecting to catch us out. Perhaps he was hoping that he could uncover all sorts of bad practices and go off with a feather in his cap. However, what he has seen is a really great team in which everyone is committed. We are honest with each other, we trust each other. And that sets the standard for the rest of the business.'

At that moment Olivia came in. With a brief, 'Hi Mum,' she headed for the hob with an appreciative sniff. 'Is that what I think it is?' she asked, looking up at Michael.

'Your favourite, unless you've changed your mind recently.'

'No way!' Olivia exclaimed, picking out one of the now golden-coloured pieces of aubergine and plopping it into her mouth. 'Yummy!'

'Hey, fingers out!' called Michael, waving a spatula, and Olivia stuck her tongue out at him and waltzed out of the kitchen.

Half an hour later Olivia was back, with Jason in tow this time and both seemingly in good spirits – which lasted throughout the meal.

'I am nominating you for the Nobel Peace Prize,' Julie-Anne told Michael once they were alone together.

'I shall go and work on my acceptance speech right away,' Michael laughed. 'And talking of speeches, shouldn't you be preparing what you are going to say tomorrow?'

'You're right,' Julie-Anne agreed. 'See you later then.'

CHAPTER 26

TOWN HALL

Even at such short notice, most people had made it into the office for Julie-Anne's Town Hall meeting, with some of the field-based staff joining electronically. Julie-Anne stood, flanked by her team, at one end of the big open-plan office.

'I have some news I want to share with you all,' she began, 'but before I do that I want you all to reflect on your performance over the last few years and where you have all come from.

'Five years ago, Rex Tillerson took over the leadership role here. I knew Rex at that time and we often talked together. So, I know what a great job Rex, and all of you, did to make this a great business, and a great place to work. I know that Rex is doing well, and he will want to know that all of you are too.

'Now we are facing very challenging times. We have had some issues with supply. We have had to overcome some challenges around packaging, and an issue that could have led to a serious breach of labelling compliance had it not been caught in time. However, the biggest challenge of all has been generics finding their way into the marketplace before our patent expiry. That hit sales very hard and is continuing to have an impact.

'As you all know, Myovilite has been a market-leading product for a long time, but the winds of change are blowing. In the US particularly, some customers have already moved to different diagnostic methods, using different technologies and different products. That is why we have been developing Axxanent. But the delays in bringing Axxanent to market have caused the organisation to seriously consider the future of Imaging. I am not going to pretend otherwise. It is possible that the decision may be to close us down,' Julie-Anne held up a finger in anticipation of a ripple of comment, 'another option might be to find a buyer for the division and we could continue under new ownership.

'Whatever the outcome may be, we,' Julie-Anne glanced to either side. Naomi and Jeff stood on her left, John and Paul to her right, 'we all think this is the most fantastic opportunity. It is an opportunity to show how good we really are, to deliver everything that is asked of us, and to do it with a level of enthusiasm and professionality that will leave people talking about us as a great business whatever the future brings.' Julie-Anne paused to gauge the reaction. One of Naomi's team, Harriet, was first to speak.

'I think we probably all appreciate what you are saying, Julie-Anne,' she paused and looked around, gaining a few nods of agreement, 'and we trust you and the team to have our best interests at heart. The thing is,' she paused again, 'what exactly is it that you want us to do differently?'

'Well,' Julie-Anne responded quickly, 'as Ted Williams would say if he were here, that is a *great* question. And that's what I am coming to next. There is no one area that jumps out where something needs fixing. It's not that simple. The problem is more one of success. We have been successful for years, so we have simply been left to get on with it. And when people and teams are successful for a long time, they tend to start neglecting the very things that made them successful in the first place. At the same time, the rules of the game are changing. Everything about Axxanent is different. We have a lot to learn, and we will have to up our game. So, two things to begin with. I, that is, we,'

Julie-Anne smiled and looked to her left and right, 'are asking everyone to do two things right away. The first is to look at your own job, your workspace, the way you interact with other people and other teams, and look for every single tiny thing we could improve.'

'Aha, you mean marginal gains!' exclaimed Tim, one of the marketing team.

'If you like, yes,' Julie-Anne said, 'but I prefer to think of it as focussing on being the best we can possibly be, by doing everything in the best way and the most efficient way. That doesn't mean we can't go on having fun at work,' she added quickly, 'in fact, I am hoping we can all have a lot of fun doing this together.'

'OK, what's the second thing?' called out Aditya, a data analyst.

'The second thing is to transform this business from being a steady state universe into an expanding one! While we set about improving everything we are doing currently, we also need to do everything possible to make sure we hit the ground running when Axxanent arrives. Instead of being afraid of that change and the disruption it might bring, let's turn those things into opportunities. Let's make sure that when we all look back on this time we say "Wow, I can't believe we did that," rather than "I wish we had done that".'

A murmur of assent spread through the room. Heads were nodding and a few quiet remarks began to turn into lively conversations.

'Well *done*!' said Jeff in heartfelt tones, and the other team members joined in with congratulating Julie-Anne. Even Paul was moved to say: 'Yes, that does seem to have gone down very well.'

'Well, let's go and join in the conversation,' said Julie-Anne, leading the way forward.

CHAPTER 27

ACTION

As the Town Hall meeting dispersed, Julie-Anne gathered her team together for a quick huddle.

'I know I said it before,' Jeff started, 'but that was brilliant! We could have lost everyone there, but you seem to have got the whole business behind you.'

'As I said, very impressive,' added Paul. Naomi and Vijay nodded their agreement.

'Well, thanks,' said Julie-Anne. 'I was trying my hardest, but there is still a lot we need to do. That may have been enough to get people on side, to move hearts and minds, but what we really need is action. We need to get people doing things that are right for the longer term, but that also provide some quick wins. Unless everyone sees positive outcomes very quickly this will all die on the vine.'

'So how do we make sure that doesn't happen?' asked Vijay.

'Plans, timetables, projects, roles and responsibilities,' answered Julie-Anne quickly. 'I think we should each own a project or workstream, and pick a cross-functional team to help deliver it.'

'Yes,' added John, 'and perhaps we should start with the three things we identified in our stories on the offsite.'

'Which were?' asked Vijay, 'remind me.'

'Sorting out meetings,' that was Paul.

'Workarounds,' added Julie-Anne.

'And combatting complacency,' said John, adding, 'not to mention hubris,' with a nod in Paul's direction.

'I'll take on meetings, if no-one has any objections to that?' said Jeff. 'I'd really love to crack the meeting culture and start to free up everyone's time.' That met with approval, and with a gleam in his eye, Paul claimed workarounds. 'I'm pretty unpopular with the whole compliance thing,' he said with a thin smile, 'but perhaps if I can show people the benefits of sticking to a system and sorting it out if it doesn't work, rather than just doing one's own thing, I may gain a few Brownie points with people.'

'I'm up for the complacency thing,' John said. 'I really liked that story, very compelling.'

'I'd like to add one to that,' Naomi responded. 'I think that we have become very set in our ways, and I think we really need to work on seeing things differently and looking at different ways of doing things. I'd like to set up a project around that.'

'What would you call it?' Julie-Anne asked.

Naomi thought for a moment before replying. 'Flexible thinking. Or perhaps Thinking Flexibly would be better – I have some good ideas about that.'

'Great,' said Julie-Anne, 'what else do we need to focus on?'

'We should look at where people work as well as how they work,' said Vijay. 'I'm not talking about taking the whole company virtual. We know that doesn't suit everyone, and quite a lot of our people like the office environment. But I am thinking back to when the building was refurbished some years ago. People had to move desks, and teams sat with people they wouldn't necessarily interact with during the day-to-day. The interesting thing was that nearly everyone said they enjoyed the experience. The variety freshened everyone up, and it was definitely good for breaking down silos and building collaborative practices.'

'It's all yours, Vijay,' Julie-Anne told him.

'And you?' Vijay asked.

'I have been thinking about that,' said Julie-Anne. 'I am going to focus my efforts on getting everybody to take action, and specifically actions that will create more opportunities and more freedom to get things done. I'll be going after anywhere we have become overly bureaucratic, and I'll be looking for increased delegation and initiative.

'The crucial thing though is to make sure that this is all about action. We need absolute clarity on roles and responsibilities, plus good timelines of course. And let's have a weekly catch-up – a stand-up huddle – to keep in touch with progress and any problems. Friday lunchtime work for everyone? We are usually all around then.

'Can I also ask that everyone does key headings and first actions for this Friday,' Julie-Anne went on.

'Sorry,' said Paul, but could you explain that?'

'I was just about to,' Julie-Anne smiled. 'I think it's probably new to everyone. What I would like to see is each project broken down into four or five main parts or headings, and under each of those, the very first action that will move that part forward. It's very important that those things are real actions, not woolly words like investigate, organise, clarify or ensure.'

John laughed out loud and said: 'That sounds like every marketing report I've ever written!'

'Which might explain a thing or two!' Jeff shot back.

'I'm not saying those words have no place in a business context,' said Julie-Anne, 'it's just that they aren't action verbs. They don't describe what you are actually going to do. Things like call, email, write or talk to are genuine actions you can take, and it's surprising how few of those things there really are. It's a great discipline and one that will definitely keep us on track.'

'What do we do when we have done that first action though?'
asked Vijay.

'Strike a line through it and write the next one,' Julie-Anne
explained. 'You can do it on a spreadsheet or on a desktop, I use a
piece of A4 paper, low tech though that may seem. You can have a
piece of paper pinned up on the wall or use a whiteboard. However
you do it, I suggest writing the big items across the top, with the
first action for each one underneath. Then you can just cross each
action off as it's completed and write the next one underneath.'

'Sounds good, I must say,' remarked Vijay.

'Ooh yes, I like that a lot,' Naomi chipped in. 'In fact, I think I
might introduce that to all the teams.'

'Interesting,' added Paul.

CHAPTER 28

PROGRESS

The first weekly huddle went well. Conducted with everyone standing up, as requested by Julie-Anne, and keeping the focus on action. Everyone came equipped with their key headings and first actions, and a list of prospective project members. The meeting was brisk with a quick summary from everyone in turn of what had been achieved so far, and some amusement as everyone tried to make sure their next action was really an action – and was the best action – under the scrutiny of the team as a whole.

Over the next couple of months, the fog of meetings that had been business as usual for so long began to clear. As well as a meeting protocol, Jeff introduced a process whereby at the beginning of any meeting, other than regular meetings of the same people, everyone briefly stated why they were there and what they wanted to get out of the meeting. He also introduced the Rule of Two Feet, which said that if you were not contributing to a meeting, or getting something of value out of it, you should use your two feet to go somewhere else and do something productive. Gradually meetings started to disappear from calendars, and those that stayed in took less time and generally involved fewer people.

Paul reported that, after a slightly shaky start, he had managed to throw off his 'Big Brother' image and was getting good cooperation in seeking out root causes and creating a willingness to fix problems rather than skirt around them.

John had become increasingly enthusiastic on finding that 'combatting complacency' had morphed over time into continuous improvement and that people were finding increased motivation from looking for ways to improve things. His project team were logging improvements made and building them into a knowledge-sharing platform, enabling people in all parts of the business to look at what other teams had done and see what might be reproducible or adaptable.

Spreading the idea of thinking flexibly was proving more of a problem according to Naomi. It was not that people were unwilling, rather that some took to it like ducks to water while other people found it difficult to generate alternatives or different concepts. Instead Naomi focussed on making sure every team had a flexible-thinking champion whose job was to ask 'Yes, and...?' whenever the team made a decision. That was shorthand for 'Yes, that's a good answer we've come up with, and what would be another, equally good, answer?' The catchphrase had taken hold and was yielding results, while some of the champions had formed an out-of-hours WhatsApp group swapping lateral-thinking puzzles with each other in friendly competition.

Vijay had done a great deal of external research, looking at different businesses and finding creative and enterprising companies only too willing to show off work environments geared to creating flexibility and maximising cooperation. He had seen everything from an old print works, with a huge atrium in the middle, used as a communal working and meeting space, to a purpose-built high-tech building housing a design company and filled with iconic pieces of design and engineering that provided inspiration and inspired curiosity at every turn. He had looked at flexible working in a number of guises, including hot desking; 'free-ranging' – working anywhere but with a given radius of a central office; squads, scrums and sprints; and flexible use of spaces including a meeting room with stackable chairs that could turn into a meditation space, and an open-plan cafeteria that transformed into a presentation hall. He was in the process of following that up with focus groups to find out how people wanted to organise themselves and their working spaces.

Julie-Anne had focussed on managers and team leaders, looking at ways to increase delegation, allocate more responsibility to individuals and strip out bureaucracy. At the same time, she had set about creating a climate across the business that encouraged people to take the initiative, and managers to manage by outputs, not by hours spent or where people were working.

All of the team's actions started to permeate the business over time. As individuals grew in confidence that they were being trusted to do their jobs, and managers began to extend their trust, Julie-Anne observed a virtuous cycle at work where improvement built on improvement. With less time spent checking up on things and requesting more and more reports, managers found themselves with time to coach, to think about the development of teams and people, and at the same time to take a more strategic view of things, all without losing sight of performance and the need to deliver.

The focus on improvement across the business, rather than just performance, generated optimism as well as creativity.

'You know, this place is really humming,' John commented to Vijay after a particularly focussed and productive meeting.

'Yes,' Vijay laughed. 'I've never worked anywhere where Marketing and Medical Affairs weren't at loggerheads – and I've known it be an all-out war in some companies.'

'But you and I have always got along, haven't we?' John protested.

'Oh, yes,' Vijay was reassuring, 'we got off on the right foot straight away, but seeing the teams working together the way they are is phenomenal and I have a hunch that it's going to get even better.'

'How so?'

'Well what's come out of all the research and focus groups on work environment is firstly that we should be working even more flexibly than we already are. Some people prefer the office environment, after all we do have a good culture here, but others would like more freedom, particularly those with young children. I spoke to one person in another company who had been there three years and she said she had never missed a school nativity play, sports day or concert – and she had never missed a performance target either.'

'Sounds like a dodgy overachiever to me!' joked John.

'No, really,' Vijay replied, 'the whole place was like that. People organised their work around their lives and really got things done. They did a lot of work on induction so that people coming in understood all the tools and technology, but just as importantly they understood the culture and expectations. They also did a lot of training so that there was a culture of continuous development, which was very motivating.'

'I would say we have a good basis for that already,' John said.

Vijay agreed: 'Yes. I think we would need more training on managing by outputs and we should look at team protocols as well as scheduling systems to make sure that people have got things covered, but overall I think we are in a good place to move in that direction. The second thing is that we should make much better use of team walls, so that everyone can see what everyone else is doing. I know we have all the KPIs on the dashboard, but this is more tactical, living in the day-to-day.'

'Well, that would certainly shake things up a bit.' John grinned. 'Be quite hard to drift back to complacency with all that going on!'

'Exactly,' said Vijay with a knowing smile.

CHAPTER 29

A WORD OF THANKS

At the end of the next quarter, Naomi came into the management meeting with a broad smile on her face. Since her financial report was the first item on the agenda, she didn't need to contain her excitement too long.

'I am delighted to tell you that for the third month running, and actually the second quarter running, we have hit forecast every month! I'm talking about the revenue forecast here of course, and I'll come back to that in a moment, but before I do…' Naomi paused and took a breath.

'I ought to say that I am excited about that for two very different reasons. The first is that by working very closely with Jeff's team,' Naomi and Jeff exchanged smiles of recognition, 'I think we have got the message right across the organisation, and particularly with sales…' a thumbs up from Jeff here, '…that what Group want us to report to them at the end of a quarter is a set of figures that exactly matches the forecast we have made.' At this Jeff nodded graciously and Naomi continued, 'I know that can be an odd message, especially to a sales force who, and I give great credit to Jeff here, always want to beat their targets, but it gives Group more confidence in us if we hit exactly the numbers we say we will. So, the first reason I am excited is that we have done exactly that, for three months in a row!'

Naomi flicked through a few slides and explained the position in more detail.

'The really exciting thing,' she continued, 'is this!' The next slide showed costs as opposed to revenues. 'While we have not only been accurately forecasting revenues and hitting those forecasts,' Naomi went on, 'we have also been reducing costs.'

'Have you been downsizing in Finance?' Paul asked, but with a light touch that caused a sudden burst laughter from the team, including Naomi.

'No,' she replied. 'It's a combination of all the things we've been putting in place over the last few months. I think as we gradually tied ourselves up in more complications, we brought in more part-time staff and more freelancers to help with the workload. No discredit to any of these people, but we were turning to external resources and however good they are, these are all people who are off the payroll and off the head count, so they are almost a hidden cost to the business.

'I think everything that Julie-Anne has put in place, with a vision of a best-in-class organisation that she has inspired us to move towards, helped us to develop and to put into action, has streamlined the business to an extraordinary degree!

'We are in line to deliver a record profit back to Group, and if that isn't an achievement in the face of adversity – I don't know what is!

'What's more, as Jeff will confirm, and I think you all know anyway, take-up of Axxanent has been much quicker and much better than we anticipated.'

'Yes,' Jeff agreed. 'It's more a question of demand chasing supply, so we have adjusted year-end forecasts up, and we are hitting all those targets.'

'What has caused that?' asked Paul.

'Well,' Jeff replied, 'the original market research showed that there might be considerable reluctance to switch. That's proved not to be the case, in most instances at least. But I also think that we were feeling defeated before we started, and that everything we have been doing since the beginning of the year has had a huge effect on morale. Although we sell a very technical product in a highly regulated industry, we still need our salespeople to be passionate about what they do, and to believe in the products, the business and their own abilities. We were losing that battle on all three fronts, now we are winning on all three.'

Paul nodded thoughtfully and then asked: 'Julie-Anne?'

'It's been a fantastic team performance,' Julie-Anne said quickly. 'Everyone has played a part, and together we have achieved more than I think any one of us thought we could.'

'I think it's due to a fantastic leadership performance,' Paul said quietly. Julie-Anne looked slightly discomforted, but Paul continued before she could say anything. 'Yes, everyone has worked very hard and played a part, but it is down to you and the way you approached things that has brought us here. And I want to make a personal point. I started out as a complete cynic. I was expecting to find all sorts of things to complain about, and actually I haven't. The business had been well run under Rex Tillerson, but it was, well perhaps moribund is too harsh, maybe a little bit set in its ways, business as usual, that sort of thing, and from there I don't believe it could have made a success of launching Axxanent and making the transition it has done.' He looked up and smiled at Julie-Anne. 'I am very admiring of your leadership, and not least because you have got me onside and feeling like part of this team. And for that, I am actually very grateful.'

CHAPTER 30

A CHRISTMAS MESSAGE

December brought snowy roads, Christmas lights and year-end figures. And an excited call from Ted Williams.

'Hey, Julie-Anne, how are you doing?' Julie-Anne was hardly able to reply before Ted went on. 'Your results have certainly caused a stir over here. Craig Houston is really excited about what you have achieved.' Craig Houston was the Group Chief Executive and had been in position for two years. He had taken over from an insular predecessor with a financial background who rarely spoke in public and was almost never interviewed. A charismatic man with a big smile and a big presence, Houston could not have been more different. As well as embarking on a series of high-profile acquisitions to strengthen the company's research base, he had been very successful in raising the profile of Incolumitas among its stakeholders, and with the public more generally, by investing in not only its businesses and its people, but in community and humanitarian projects too. He was a well-known figure in the industry, and well liked in the business.

'Well that's great...' Julie-Anne started to say, but Ted carried on.

'So much so that he wants to meet you. He's planning on flying over next week.'

'Goodness! He can't be coming all that way just to say well done. Are they still going to sell us off and he wants to tell me in person?' That didn't seem likely, but it was all Julie-Anne could think of in the moment of surprise.

'Hell, no,' Ted laughed. 'He wants to find out precisely how you turned it around. He's intrigued.'

CHAPTER 31

A WISE MAN FROM THE WEST

Craig Houston was a big man. He was tall, blond haired and lightly freckled. He had very wide hands, Julie-Anne's finger barely went around his knuckles as they shook hands, but his smile was genuine and there was no doubting the warmth of his greeting.

'I make no secret of the fact that a little while ago there was a considerable lobby to sell off the whole Imaging division,' he began as they settled down. 'It was underperforming, it was non-core,' he paused and chuckled, 'and for some people there were a whole lot of other things it either was or wasn't. However, I have never believed that the numbers tell the whole story of a business.' At which point he held his right hand up, palm outwards. 'Not that I am saying the numbers don't matter; I know that you're fully aware of just how much they matter.' He went on. 'So, I was minded to make that move to sell it off, and I was thinking about explaining that to Rex, as well as to Ah Cy Siong in Asia Pacific and to Danny Raynor back home. Then Ted told me about Rex, and you know Julie-Anne, that really should not have made any difference to my decision-making process, but somehow, on a gut feel, it did. I didn't feel that Ah Cy had been in post long enough to make an impact in Asia Pacific. The US had not been doing well, but I believed in Danny and I believed that with good support he could turn things around, and I am pleased to say that he is doing that. But the thing is,' he paused, clasping his hands in front of him and leaning forward in his seat, 'neither of them has produced anything near as dramatic as your turnaround here in Europe. So, what I want to know,' the broad expansive smile broke out again, 'is how, if you'll pardon my language, in the hell have you done it?'

Julie-Anne took a deep breath. 'Well,' she said, 'I have been on something of a journey myself here, and recently I spent some time thinking about that.

'The first thing I realised was that the business didn't have a vision, something it was striving to become, or move towards. It occurred to me that unless you are taking a group of people somewhere they have not been before, or building something that doesn't exist yet, you are probably not really leading anything. So, vision was the first thing.

'That got me to thinking about visionaries, because the world is full of people with a vision, who aren't being leaders. I realised that leadership is about creating a vision *and* inspiring people to want to come with you in pursuit of that vision. So, I made something of a study of inspirational behaviours, being positive, being a radiator of energy, not a drain, even when you don't feel like it. Encouraging other people to believe and be confident in themselves as well as in the business.'

'I certainly get all of that,' Houston agreed. 'Vision and inspiration, but why do I have the feeling you are going to tell me more?'

'Because there's more to tell?' Julie-Anne smiled and went on. 'One thing I have noticed about some other businesses, particularly ones much younger than ours, is that they have a vision, which inspires everyone, and inspires them to leap into action – which is great, until a few years later when they end up herding cats.' Craig Houston guffawed at that and nodded as Julie-Anne continued, 'or in one case I remember someone saying to me: "The problem we have here is that this is a business founded by entrepreneurs, so everybody wants to be an entrepreneur, and then we end up with a highly regulated business being run largely by a bunch of mavericks."'

'Which is most definitely somewhere you do not want to be,' Houston agreed.

'Right,' Julie-Anne went on, 'and the missing piece in that over-rapid journey is development. After all, if you are building something that doesn't exist yet, or taking people to somewhere they haven't been before, it's almost a certainty that you're going to need to develop some additional capabilities in order to get there.'

'Right – so you are talking people development here?'

'Yes, first and foremost, but it actually encompasses the development of all the capabilities the business requires: processes, systems, financing, plant, whatever it might be.

'And the last part, and I am sure you know this better than me, Craig, is that leaders need to be very good at getting themselves and others into action. Not just any action, but specific, focussed actions that move us closer to achieving the vision.'

Craig Houston sat back in his seat with a broad grin on his face. 'Well I'll be damned,' he said. 'I majored in Management Science and Engineering at one the best universities in the US, and I have an MBA from an even more prestigious institution, but I think you have said more about leadership, in fewer words, than I have heard anywhere before in my whole business career.'

'Vida!' said Julie-Anne with a laugh and a note of triumph.

'Excuse me?' Houston leaned forward, looking puzzled.

'Vision, Inspiration, Development, Action!' Julie-Anne told him. 'That's my mantra. It spells VIDA. Which also, happily, means "life" in Spanish,' she added.

'Vida,' Craig Houston repeated slowly. 'I get it. That is good. No, wait a minute, that is very good!' He paused, grinned and thought for a moment. 'You know, Julie-Anne, what I would really like is for you to come to the January conference in New York and make a presentation about VIDA and how you have used it here. I think you are really on to something, and I want everyone in this business to be a VIDA leader!'

CHAPTER 32

TRAVELLING FAR

'So, you are off to the States, well, well!' was Michael's comment when he heard the news.

'Actually, I had a slightly different idea,' Julie-Anne grinned back at him.

'Really? And what might that be?' Michael asked.

'I thought *we* might go to the States.'

'You mean just you and me? Second honeymoon?'

It was Michael's turn to grin, but Julie-Anne burst out laughing.

'Sorry to disappoint but that wasn't what I was thinking. I meant all of us! A family holiday in the Big Apple; Olivia can visit Beverley, Jason can see her brother Johnny, and we can spend some time with Bob and Margaret.'

'Wow!' Michael exclaimed. 'You're moving fast. What's brought this on?'

'Simple,' Julie-Anne told him. 'I came up with a **vision** of doing this together in a way that will hopefully help Livvy and Jason to get over Beverley and Johnny moving away. I think I can make that sound enticing enough to give them some **inspiration**. A trip to New York should broaden minds and help their **development**. Now all I need to do is get into **action** to make the arrangements!'

PART 2:

THE VIDA WAY OF LEADERSHIP

In truth, Julie-Anne did not invent the VIDA model. It has its origins in some highly respected and validated research into leadership behaviours that promote, and are predictive of, high performance.

That research was conducted by Professor Harold M. Schroder who was Professor of Psychology at Princeton University, and subsequently Professor of Management at the University of South Florida. Originally published as *Managerial Competence: The Key to Excellence*, the work was further developed by Dr Tony Cockerill and others at London Business School.

The behaviours identified by the research can be helpfully clustered together. While these four 'clusters' are usually named Thinking, Developmental, Inspirational and Action behaviours, they align perfectly with a simple and practical way to think about what leading means and how to develop leadership in individuals and organisations. This simple alignment is VIDA:

- Vision
- Inspiration
- Development
- Action

Let's look at each of those in turn.

VISION

It is important to understand the place and purpose of vision, and the visioning processes that might be used to create one. A vision is not a replacement for strategy, nor for scenario planning. The objective of a vision is to create a highly desirable future state, one which attracts people to be a part of the endeavour to make it real, and which creates engagement and alignment around the common goal. Julie-Anne recognised that and set about using a disciplined process to create a vision with her leadership team.

Three key behaviours underpin the creation of an inspiring leadership vision. The first is gathering information. If you do not know what is going on, then the chances of coming up with something that is already old are very high in the current environment. The essence of gathering information is to search widely across a broad range of sources – and not necessarily ones that have an obvious connection with your business, or the areas of your current thinking. The first exercise Julie-Anne uses (the seven questions in chapter seven) is designed to get people to locate information from a wide variety of sources and viewpoints.

The second behaviour involved in creating a vision is called concept formation. The essence of forming powerful new concepts (and a good vision fits squarely within that definition) is linking ideas. Theodore Zeldin, philosopher, sociologist, historian and writer declared that 'All invention and progress come from finding a link between two ideas that have never met.' The key is bringing together pieces of information and ideas from different places. Julie-Anne uses the 'spider's web' or 'pizza pie' chart to do this in chapter nine.

The third vital 'thinking behaviour' Julie-Anne encourages (in chapter eleven) is flexible thinking. This is rare, but people who do it have trained themselves to become very good at forming a second choice, an alternative vision, solution or course of action that is every bit as good as the first one they came up with. This concept is beautifully captured in a phrase coined by Roger von Oech in *A Whack on the Side of the Head*; he talks about finding 'the second right answer.' To fully exemplify this behaviour the team could have come up with two different but equally valuable visions, and then compared the pros and cons of each, possibly combining them into an overarching vision superior to either of the original proposals.

INSPIRATION

The lone visionary is an archetypical figure – and usually a tragic one. It's a world of 'listen to me' or 'I told you so'. Leadership requires more, and we use the term Inspiration to cover everything a leader needs to do to build followership. That is, to get enough people engaged in wanting to make the vision real to at least get things moving in the right direction.

A rich body of research in the area of leadership has examined the influence of inspirational leadership on employees' motivation, attitudes and behaviours. While 'charismatic' leadership has generally fallen from favour, the role of inspirational behaviours has risen in prominence, especially the importance of inspirational leaders, who through their relationships with team members can foster attitudes vital for performance in geographically dispersed settings. The new world of work is showing that inspirational behaviours are important in all contexts, but that their importance is highlighted where virtual teams are concerned. In fact, inspirational leadership behaviours are a good predictor of individuals' trust in their fellow team members, and their commitment to the team, which in turn are good predictors of performance and results. We are concerned here with three different behaviours: presentation, influencing and building confidence.

When we talk about inspirational behaviour most people initially think of what might better be defined as platform speaking. In fact, the first behaviour covers all communication, the essence of which is being able to get your message across, both clearly and concisely. What you say needs to be well-structured. Whether it is to an audience, a board meeting or an individual, you need to have the basics in place – good eye contact and minimal distractions. It is vital that you communicate your key ideas with economy and clarity. Julie-Anne's Town Hall talk in chapter twenty-six does exactly that, and these are skills which can be taught and learned, such that even very poor presenters can be coached to become very competent.

Showing that you mean what you say is vital, but so is how you put that message across. You need to command the attention and interest of the audience. Whether you do that using technology, visual aids, gestures, voice modulation, humour or analogies might depend on personal preference and style; Julie-Anne chose to speak from her heart. However you do it, when the chips are down you need to make it as compelling and gripping as a great movie.

It almost goes without saying that influence is a critical leadership behaviour. John Kotter's study *What Leaders Really Do* provides an insight into understanding how important this behaviour is. In trying to make sense of how CEOs of gigantic corporations were actually achieving anything when, as Kotter observed through work-shadowing, no conversation seemed to last more than five minutes and no concentrated periods of time were spent on one topic, Kotter reached a brilliant conclusion. He deduced that each of these leaders firstly had an Agenda – the four or five key things they really felt they needed to achieve.

Now, here is where influence comes in. None of these executives was telling people what to do to achieve the outcomes they wanted. Each of them had perfected the art of working out the first action necessary to move that agenda item one step forward. The tool they used to do that was influence, and they were adept at getting buy-in, building strong alliances and win-win outcomes.

The third inspirational behaviour is building confidence. It is an interesting behaviour because you must build a base for it, and that base is the making of timely decisions. These are not snap decisions that may leave people thinking you acted too hastily, or delayed decisions that send a negative message that you are indecisive. Moreover, the essence of building confidence is about demonstrating your own belief in and high expectations for the success of a particular plan or strategy. Julie-Anne is determined that the business can succeed, never wavers in that belief, and continually expresses it.

DEVELOPMENT

It is well documented that most start-ups that fail do not lack an idea; anyone who starts a business must have some vision, even if it is rather vague. New futures and things-that-don't-exist-yet nearly always require the development of new capabilities. Unless we start building in that development right at the beginning, the lack of it will catch up with us and catch us out at some point. Julie-Anne's observation of that point is taken from several real-life case studies.

As Julie-Anne says, in the widest sense development can encompass everything the business will need and that it does not already possess. But alongside systems, processes and technology, developing people is fundamental. In a command and control environment, the main desire is to get people to do exactly what they are told to do, no more and no less. As soon as you start to put more fluid and responsive structures in place, you generate a need for people to become more flexible and more creative, in terms of thinking about what they are doing and how to do it better. That generates a need for systems thinking and collaborative behaviours.

The first investment is in teamwork, which places emphasis on facilitating how team members interact with each other. High-performing leaders are adept not only at equalising the 'airtime' of different group members, but at facilitating dialogue between them so they see the connections and similarities between their ideas or options. This is a profoundly different approach to the usual one of allowing debate, discussion and 'conflict of ideas' to mill around the room. The process that Julie-Anne uses in chapter twenty-four is deliberately designed to facilitate this type of interaction between team members.

The second developmental behaviour is concerned with building a climate of trust, understanding and openness; one in which people are valued for saying what they really think, feel and believe and can do so without fear of criticism, judgement or punishment. This gets more people into the conversation, widens the spread of ideas, generates speed and cuts costs. Julie-Anne doesn't sugar coat the truth, and answers questions honestly in the Town Hall meeting. She seeks to build trust in the leadership team and to value all contributions, eventually even getting Paul onside in this way.

Finally, in developing the capabilities of people, great leaders recognise that people will only realise their true potential in supportive and developmental environments that enhance their capabilities and challenge them to do more. The role of the leader is to build that environment and to create ways for others to coach, mentor, train, provide recognition and give constructive performance feedback.

ACTION

Action is probably the area in which leaders or would-be leaders need the least personal help or development. The challenge is ensuring you are taking the right action and getting other people into action in the right ways. The key point is the extent to which you can reduce the constraints on people to enhance their freedom to act and broaden their scope to use initiative – these are the areas that Julie-Anne focusses on. Other examples would include redefining the boundaries of a market or industry, moving decision points further down the organisation by empowering people to think and decide for themselves, and giving more responsibility to the people closest to customers. When the organisation at large is being proactive, this is evidenced by people going around obstacles, and if they can't go around, going over, under or even straight through!

Beyond this, the key question for many of today's leaders is simply 'Are we adding value?' Adding value involves building a culture in which everyone is encouraged to focus activity and processes on adding value to the customer. This achieved prominence in Ranjay Gulati's book *Reorganize for Resilience: Putting Customers at the Center of Your Business.* His research explored leadership and strategic challenges for building high-growth organisations in turbulent markets. Between 2001 and 2007, Gulati tracked highly customer-centric organisations and showed that they delivered shareholder returns of 150%, while the S&P 500 delivered a comparatively slender 14%.

IN CONCLUSION

The contribution of leadership to organisational performance is now well documented. VIDA provides a clear framework of learnable behaviours and sets out a practical four-part behavioural code for achieving great leadership. Adopting and practising the VIDA model and the core behaviours underpinning it enables strong leadership to be developed at any and every level in organisations, and this will ultimately drive success.

ACKNOWLEDGEMENTS

My thanks first and foremost are to friends and colleagues from the Centre for High Performance Development and all the great work that was done there to take the Schroder model into client organisations with tremendous success. That work also provided wonderful access to a huge variety of leaders in every sphere of industry, the professions and the public sector, who taught me much. On a personal level I want in particular to thank Ali Gill, now CEO at Crelos, for being a highly inspirational leader and a good friend.

I thank all of my Vybrant colleagues for their tremendous efforts in continuing to take the ideas and concepts forward and all the Vybrant associates who have contributed energy, ideas, creative thinking and brilliant suggestions directly or indirectly to the development of *The Four Fixations of a Brilliant Leader*. Among many wonderful Vybrant clients have been some truly exceptional leaders and it has been a privilege to work alongside Hester Larkin, Geoff Inskip, Ian Meakins and Richard Lees among many others, all of whom have shaped these ideas to some degree and, without knowing it at the time, added to the development of Julie-Anne's story.

Once again thanks to Heather Codling, Julie Goodwin, Anthony Sheldon and Russell Houghton for unfailing support and enthusiasm, Abi Layton for improving my prose, and my wife Pam for keeping the ship going while I tap away at my keyboard.

Last but by no means least, huge thanks to Clare Christian, Heather Boisseau and Lizzie Lewis at RedDoor Press, not only for enthusiastically supporting this project, but also for all their help in making my first business fable *The Six Conversations of a Brilliant Manager* an Amazon bestseller.

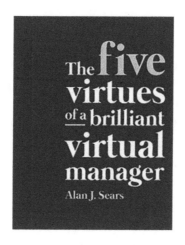

THE FIVE VIRTUES OF A BRILLIANT VIRTUAL MANAGER

CHAPTER 1: ONE DAY IN VIENNA

Roxanne Leonard took her seat opposite her boss in Vienna. The meeting rooms at Vanninmed were all named after cities in which the company had premises. Most meetings took place in open areas around the building so the request to meet in Vienna told Roxanne straight away that something was in the air.

Dan Lepada greeted her with a smile but she had known him long enough to detect the frown behind it.

'Hi Roxanne,' he began, 'thanks for coming in.'

'Are you OK, Dan?' she asked.

'Oh yeah, sure,' Dan told her. 'We have a bit of a problem, but I think I have a solution to it.'

'And the solution, I am guessing,' Roxanne smiled, flashing her very white teeth, 'involves me. Right?'

Dan barked a short laugh. 'You're way ahead of me!' he admitted.

'And, so…?' Roxanne knew the power of a pause and just waited until Dan carried on.

'Well, here's the thing. Apart from your part of it, which is working well, and that by the way is why we are having this conversation, Customer Service is just not working. We are now getting complaints from customers about our complaints procedures, can you believe? Customers are saying they aren't getting answers, or if they do they get contradictory ones, or they are passed around from person to person, saying "Oh I'll put you through…" it's like we have more silos in Customer Services than in all the rest of the business put together.'

Dan sat back and took a deep breath, then went on in more measured tones.

'Now I realise that some of this is because people don't have the information they need at their fingertips, and they can't always get it. That's part of the problem. We have to sort out a lot of internal systems and procedures as well as dealing properly with our customers concerns. Then we need to get the feedback loops working properly so that if we do get something wrong we learn from it and don't make the same mistake again.'

'Okaaay,' Roxanne smiled across the desk, 'and you are telling me this because…?'

Dan looked up. 'Because we are going to be doing things very differently from now on. We are going to get everyone onto the same system and set up a follow-the-sun model. That is going to mean coordinating here with New York, Mumbai, Singapore and Melbourne. And the person I want to do that is you.'

Roxanne's mouth opened in surprise. She shut it again without saying anything then took a breath.

'Dan I'm flattered, I really am,' she said at last 'but I don't think I'm qualified to do that. I've never run a virtual team, let alone a global operation with different cultures in different time zones.'

'Roxanne, you've worked in the Middle East, you ran New Zealand for three years and you've spent a good deal of time in the US operation. No-one is better qualified than you to see this done right.' Dan came back at her.

'That's true, but it's different. Besides what will the others think?'

'Well this may surprise you but I have spoken to Blake in New York and Arjun in Mumbai, and they are both up for it.'

'And Mitchie in Singapore?'

'Mitchie has been telling me that she doesn't get as much support as she would like reporting into the region, and of course Liam in Melbourne has only just joined, and that was on the basis that things might be reorganised.'

'Hmm,' Roxanne pursed her lips. 'It sounds as though this is pretty much a done deal.'

'It only needs you to say yes,' Dan told her with a grin.

ABOUT THE AUTHOR

ALAN SEARS is an author, coach and leadership consultant. For the last fifteen years he has headed up Vybrant Organisation Ltd, a consultancy specialising in leadership, management and top team development. He has worked with thousands of leaders and managers, from FTSE 100 companies to SMEs and start-ups, the public sector and not-for-profit organisations.

alanjsears.com

alanjsears.com/four-fixations-brilliant-leader-book/

@alanjsears

Linkedin: Alan J Sears (linkedin.com/in/alsears/)

To find out more about Alan Sears, or sign up for email
updates about new books, visit

alanjsears.com

You can get in touch with Alan via:

 @alanjsears

 Alan J Sears

Find out more about RedDoor Press and sign up
to our newsletter to hear about our latest releases,
author events, blog tours, exciting competitions,
cover reveals and book trailers at

reddoorpress.co.uk

YOU CAN ALSO FOLLOW US:

 @RedDoorBooks

 Facebook.com/RedDoorPress

 @reddoorbooks

Red Door